THERE'S ALWAYS
RISK IN MOVEMENT

THERE'S ALWAYS RISK IN MOVEMENT

· ·

TALES FROM OLD READING TOWN

ALAN CROFT

To order additional copies of this book, contact:
Xlibris
800-056-3182
www.Xlibrispublishing.co.uk
Orders@Xlibrispublishing.co.uk
772627

CONTENTS

Chapter 1   Chasing Waterfalls.....................................1

Chapter 2   The Wrath of the Big Ginger.....................18

Chapter 3   The Turkey and the Elusive Mouse..........27

Chapter 4   The Burning Anglia 42

Chapter 5   Belfast Hooligan..49

Chapter 6   Tears and Laughter 55

Chapter 7   Michael Bashes the Midget........................60

Chapter 8   Out of the Frying Pan and into Jesse 68

Chapter 9   Ian the Hedgehog.....................................77

Chapter 10   Tussles and Brussels..................................83

Chapter 11   Alan Ball Loves Scampi.............................89

Chapter 12   Money Down the Drain.............................97

Chapter 13   An Inviting Slice of Cheese.....................104

Chapter 14   Lily Brown's, Rebecca's, and Biggles 115

Chapter 15   Skating for a Fish Supper........................124

Chapter 16   Three in a Bed in Paris 141

Chapter 17   I Must Have Been Walking Backwards.... 150

Chapter 18   The Abduction of the Lonely Printer 160

Chapter 19   A Dead Polish Woman in Baker Street 170

Chapter 20   A Dog Called Bollox................................179

Chapter 21   The Yugoslavian Pie Fight 188

Chapter 22   A Fishy Caper on Kings Road...................194

Chapter 23   Red Heels in the Sahara..........................202

Chapter 24   The Spanish Expedition 209

Chapter 25   Heathens to the Right 217

Chapter 26   The Final Whistle 233

For my mother-in-law, Ena Wilson. Unforgettable.

Thanks for the memories of those others who have passed away:

- Simon Denning
- Mickey Donaldson
- Richard Downs
- Keith Harper
- Jimmy Maloney
- Marty O'Neill
- Rob Rose
- Stefan Roszczyk
- Maggie (Hunter) Wise.

ACKNOWLEDGEMENTS

Upon completion of this follow-up to *Belfast: Tears and Laughter*, one thing has always been a constant: the love and support of my mother and father. Without them, I would have struggled to accomplish anything. They made my good days better and helped my bad days disappear. Although we have been apart for so long, my parents' presence has always been with me. They instilled their goodness in my sister and me, which ultimately protected us during the dark days of the Ulster Troubles. My sister, Kathleen, has helped me to no end by being the rock behind the family that I left behind.

A special thank you goes to my wife, Nancy, for allowing the publication of *There's Always Risk in Movement*. She was a witness to most of the interesting escapades and could have easily slapped me about and pulled the plug on the book. Also, thanks to my sons—Sam, for his knowledge and advice and for editing the book, and Bobby, just for being Bobby. Thanks too to Jacqueline Casbolt for suggesting the title, *There's Always Risk in Movement*, and to Jerry Nicholls for providing the photos for the cover page.

Of course, I would be negligent if I didn't acknowledge the part that the people of Reading played in making it easy to complete this book. Whether they were close friends or just a selection of oddball characters who casually crossed my path, I'm grateful to them all. The biggest pleasure I found when writing this memoir was being able to return to that time in my mind and relive it for a second time. It was magical. Thank you.

INTRODUCTION

As the years pressed forwards at a relentless pace, I contemplated what had motivated the decisions that I had made to direct me along the erratic road of life. The passage of time that began with a near-perfect childhood moved on to a volatile adolescence and finally brought me to where I am now. As with everyone's journey, each last-minute change of heart or mind will be conclusive in establishing which path they will eventually take. I thought of the countless people I had encountered during that period and how they influenced me in one way or another.

Life is certainly not linear. It is made up of a series of moments woven together into mundane or poignant patterns. These cycles and circumstances ultimately determine who we really are and who we become. If you reach that later phase of life with a feeling of contentment, then it will almost certainly have had to do with the paths that were taken and who walked them with you. The direction of my life was to change one winter's evening in a smoke-filled Belfast social club.

Just before my twentieth birthday a certain Oliver Major provided me with an intervention. He convinced me I was on the road to nowhere and that I would arrive there soon. He suggested that I should leave my troublesome homeland to join him on a casual adventure to the town of Reading. He explained that I would say goodbye to the grey skies of Ulster and welcome the blue horizons of southern England. Although the move would officially be to a different part of the same country, it ultimately proved to be worlds apart.

The Reading years undoubtedly rewarded me with some of the best days of my life, and I acknowledge that the great friends I made there were a significant reason for that. Our strong bond was second to none. The pleasure of having shared such grand times with these unique people allows me to reminisce about my past with great fondness. As time passes, new acquaintances will enter and leave your life and inevitably some of these people will become good friends. Rarely will they thoroughly understand how you became the person who you are today.

The following account is a recollection of events that began in July 1977, when I left Northern Ireland for a new life in England. I would find that the transition from a culture of violence and political strife to one of peaceful accord was pleasantly uncomplicated. Ultimately, this is not only my story but all of ours: a documentation portraying the lives of a group of youths riding the crest of the wave to see where it would end.

CHAPTER 1

CHASING WATERFALLS

Manchester United's manager Tommy Docherty had just been dramatically sacked after he allegedly shagged the wife of the club's physiotherapist. He certainly went out with a bang following a famous 2–1 victory over Liverpool in the FA Cup final two months earlier. Hot Chocolate was the chart topper with 'So You Win Again' and the Sex Pistols had impeded the Silver Jubilee celebrations for Queen Elizabeth II by blasting out their rendition of 'God Save the Queen' from a boat on the River Thames.

It was July 1977, and the short journey from Heathrow to Reading along the M4 was smooth and precise as the coach approached the large roundabout at Sutton Seeds. It was early afternoon, and the long trek from Belfast was almost over. After receiving slaps to the ear lugs courtesy of Beaker's sweaty hand, Liam and I were wakened from our slumber and caught our first glimpse of the fabled town. Beaker— named after the playful owl, Ollie Beak, a character from a children's daytime classic TV show from the 1960s—had lived in Reading before. He had become a legend in his own mind as he had made a name for himself with his raunchy guitar playing as part of a band called Banshee, which enjoyed success around the local pubs in the early 1970s.

Music was the main attraction of the trip, with the upcoming Reading Festival (one of the largest of its type in Britain) top of the agenda. We'd planned to hang around for a while after the festival with the hope of picking up some work. Michael, another pal, was due to arrive a couple of weeks later just before the big show began. Beaker had arranged to meet big Tom to help us find suitable accommodation on our first night in Reading. He was also from our hometown and had played in Banshee along with Beaker but had remained in England. Michael and Tom knew each other well as they had been next-door neighbours growing up; I also knew him, but we were only casually acquainted. Liam and I were both anxious and excited by what lay ahead in the place dubbed by Beaker as *the tropical part of southern England.* He had gone into detail, describing the waterfall that cascaded over cragged rocks before entering a crystal clear pool in the town centre. On hot summer days, some refreshing ambient spray cooled passers-by.

We would soon be enjoying carefree afternoons with cold lagers on the lush green banks of the Thames as the luxury yachts rolled along on their way to Oxford, Windsor, and other exotic locations. Beautiful English girls, who outnumbered the men in Reading, would fall at our feet, mesmerised by our hypnotic Belfast accents. That being said, a quick glance at some of Beaker's previous conquests—a list which included Wine Bottle Liz, Skinny Malinky, and Stud in the Nose—did not paint a pretty picture of the available women in waiting. It would not be long before we were disappointed. Liam imagined Stud in the Nose as being a really ugly girl with a busted-in face as he thought that someone had stood on her nose (stood would be pronounced *stud* with a broad Belfast accent). When we met her, we discovered that she was indeed ugly, but she didn't have a caved-in face.

We watched with great anticipation as the coach entered Reading. It did not look good. The immediate surrounding streets of the area known as Newtown were certainly not new and looked just like the Falls Road in Belfast, only inhabited by ethnic minorities.

Minutes later, after passing the aptly named Cemetery Junction, the coach swerved aggressively into the path of oncoming taxis and local buses as they filtered out en route to their different destinations. It slowed to a crawl upon entering the central transport hub of Reading Station. The dirty old town centre was notable only for the handful of concrete high-rises which surrounded the busy train station, where natives scurried like soldier ants to and from the platforms. We quickly observed that our arrival to the tropical part of England seemed to be void of any waterfalls or lush river banks. Darkness abruptly replaced the mix of sun and clouds as the coach ducked into an exhaust fume-filled bus station crammed underneath the ground level.

With a screech of the brakes, the coach jolted to a halt; then the driver bellowed out in a strong Wurzel-like West Country accent, 'This is Reading. Everybody off!'

It was a free-for-all as the impatient passengers grabbed frantically at the luggage compartment so that they could find their cases and be on their way. Liam and I had packed a large suitcase each with the hope we would be hanging around for a while. Beaker had a canvas bag slung over his shoulder with just enough clobber to last the weekend.

My knowledge of Reading was limited. I knew that the football team had been relegated to the fourth division the previous season under the guidance of Charlie Hurley and that Maurice Evans had taken over the helm. Also, I'd heard that the team's nickname was *the Biscuitmen*, a moniker that certainly did not exude athleticism. That was all I had on the old and greying town.

'Oy, Beaker, you've been talking aul shite. This place is a dump. Exotic part of England, my arse!' said Liam, shaking his head.

'Just up this stairway is a high-class wine bar with beautiful waitresses that will tend to your every need, bringing all sorts of high-class liquors to our table. They leave the bottle with you, just like the cowboys,' Beaker replied.

'Aye, high-class liquors my ballicks. I want a pint of Guinness,' I moaned, none too impressed.

After negotiating the hazards of piss-stained beggars and dog shit on a couple of dank flights of stairs, we reached the main level at the front entrance of Cherry's Wine Bar. The unconvincing beginning of the new adventure at last seemed brighter as we entered the acceptable surroundings of an elegant wine bar and heard 'Lido Shuffle' by Boz Scaggs echoing from the jukebox. Beaker was immediately acknowledged by a funny-looking wee man with a strange accent, who minced out from behind the bar.

'What about ye, Tony? These are my two mates, Alan and Liam, and we were wondering if we could leave our cases behind the bar until we found somewhere to stay,' said Beaker confidently.

'No problem at all, my friend,' Tony replied, rubbing his hands together gleefully as he gazed at Beaker's unshaven face as if he were a long-lost lover.

'Dead on there, wee man, and could you send a couple of bottles of vino over to the table in the corner?' Beaker responded as we dumped our baggage at Tony's feet in front of the bar.

'Who's that poof?' said Liam as we slouched back into the pine chairs with mouths as dry as camels' arses.

'He's the landlord, originally from Cork and not a bad lad. Our bags will be OK here for a while,' said Beaker.

Then right on cue, a pretty bar wench delivered two cold bottles of Blue Nun to the table.

Maybe Beaker was not talking shite after all, I thought. *Reading doesn't seem so bad.*

We kicked back in preparation for a long session, feeling quite relaxed and at ease, free from soldier spot checks and searches and the possibility of the pub blowing up. After about six more Blue Nuns and the odd Pernod, my belly began to rumble and churn over. It felt like the time for a good boke, so I skidded into the toilets to discharge a much-needed technicolor yawn.

Then the unexpected occurred. A bell rang, and someone shouted out, 'Last orders please!'

Panic and fear ran through my veins. I hurried back to the table. 'What's he on about, Beaker? Is he mad? Tell him to shut up. It's only twenty past two,' I said.

'Oh aye, I forgot to tell you. The pubs in England close in the afternoon from half two until half five,' responded Beaker.

'What kind of uncivilised place is this? You can't close a bar down in the middle of the day! What are we going to do?' continued Liam, flustered and twitching at the thought of being evicted on to the street.

But he was correct. It was the law of the land unlike in Belfast, where the pubs stayed open all day. Beaker tried to reassure us that we could get a carry-out and lounge by the pond of the nearby Forbury Gardens with a few beers until the pub opened up again. Our spirits were lifted somewhat when we were informed of a Sunday drinking session to come for a mere two hours, from 12 p.m. to 2 p.m.—not long but something that wasn't available in our hometown. Before heading out into the bright afternoon sun, we still had time to get a pint of crème de menthe down our necks.

Three hours passed comfortably as we used the intermission to knock back a few lagers and catch up with some snooze time as we lay amongst visiting families and other well-dressed hoboes who frequented the park. Tom was to meet us at 7 p.m. in Cherry's Wine Bar, so there was still time for a pint in the Railway Tavern, the Mitre, and the Britannia—nice little pubs indeed. Liam and I would soon meet a lot of people as Beaker's friends from his previous visits also made their way to Cherry's. Before Tom arrived, we were introduced to Big Jonesy, who was a cricket player, and looking at him, one would say a very slow cricket player. At the same table were Jimmy and Martin, two brothers from the Republic of Ireland who sounded like the Flower Pot Men, and a fellow from Hartlepool called Jed, who sounded just like the brothers. Without doubt, these were a strange mixture of animated oddballs. Meeting different sorts was new territory for us, especially for me as the crowd I hung around with across the water were all exactly alike. They were all born in the same area, and their forefathers were white Ulster Scottish Protestants. The bar soon began to fill up, but we were lucky to have VIP seats reserved thanks to the foresight of Tony, the landlord.

Beaker seemed to be very popular in old Reading town; either that or he owed a lot of people money because the crowd that turned out to welcome him was ever increasing. He'd told us that a few of his friends from back home still lived in Reading; some of them already knew Liam. Tom eventually arrived with former Banshee members, Marty, another ex-Belfast boy, and Steve, a self-described strawberry-blonde lad, the first local we had met. Steve was one of four brothers of Glasgow descent and was really a ginger and not a strawberry blonde at all. Marty had been one of the first from my area to move to Reading, following his brother Gerry, who worked for the local newspaper. As the evening progressed and the bar began to become overcrowded, Tom suggested we move on to another pub to meet up with a few more former Belfast boys.

From the stylish expanse of Cherry's Wine Bar, we ducked to enter the Nag's Head, a pokey wee place in Russell Street packed with foul-smelling navvies straight off assorted building sites. There was not a woman to be seen. In a dark corner of the smoke-filled pub sat the three we were to meet. Danny, a muscle-bound ex-boxer, rose to greet Beaker with a firm handshake. His younger brother, Bobby, a bearded stumpy version of Danny, also left his seat to offer a similar handshake. Finally, we met Sam, an old-school pal of Bobby's who was not well known to Beaker. He was a rotund curly-haired specimen, and he seemed rather uninterested that we had joined his company. He concentrated only on his pint of lager, which he knocked down his neck in one swift movement. He spluttered, finished the move off with an earthy burp, and then rallied with a watery fart that echoed across the wooden bench and sent a putrid aroma wafting towards us.

He shouted, 'Get out and walk, ya bastard ye!'

'Aw right there, Beaker big man? Excuse Sam but he's a pig and you can't educate pork,' said Bobby.

'No problem, Bobby. These are my two mates from back home, Liam and Alan,' said Beaker. So that was it for the formalities, and we circled to down a few more pints to finish the night off. The craic was good with the laughter and banter.

It was sporadically interrupted by Sam standing up and spreading his arms high and wide to exclaim, 'I'm fuckin' airlocked! I'm fuckin' airlocked!' He was letting everyone know that he was indeed quite drunk.

Before the night was through, Bobby had managed to land me a bit of work: cash in the hand with a building company starting on Monday morning. Employment in Belfast was very difficult to come by, with 25 per cent of the workforce on the dole, so it was a bonus to get a job on the first day in England.

We split with the other three at the junction of Russell Street and Baker Street after a good session in the dingy pub. Beaker headed off to the sanctuary of Tom's modest terraced house in Field Road, but for Liam and me, it was a different story. Following some loose directions from Tom to find overnight accommodation, we negotiated our way to 40 Baker Street to meet with the unknown occupant. After kicking a few tins and the odd cat up in the air, we reached the darkened destination.

'Looks like there's no one in,' I said.

'What's the geezer called that is supposed to put us up?' asked Liam.

'I think it's Greg. Let's bang on the door,' I said, swaying a little at arm's length from the house entrance.

Liam rapped his knuckles on the wooden frame, and the old door creaked open to reveal a long shadowy hallway.

'It's pitch-black. There's definitely nobody in.' I groaned, completely wiped out.

'Who cares? I'm knackered. Let's just go on in,' said Liam, also ready to collapse as he shoved the door fully open. We shuffled down the hallway, flicking at the switches and trying to get some lights to work, but we were in the dark.

'Somebody hasn't paid their bill. The electrics been cut off,' I said.

Cautiously we made our way up a stairway to the main living room with the expectation that a mad axe murderer might jump out and hack us to pieces at any moment. The silhouette of a settee and chair were outlined by the glare of a street lamp in front of the house. We nodded to each other in agreement that the coast was clear and that it was safe to have a kip. To keep warm, we removed a pair of curtains from the large sash windows to use as blankets before calling it a night.

The next morning, I woke up with a pounding headache and struggled to my feet as I tried to recall the previous night's activities.

Liam groaned as he slowly came around. 'Argh, where are we?'

He held his hands in front of his face in an effort to block the strong sunbeam that lit us up like two mannequins in a shop window. We unfurled the curtains that we had draped over our distorted bodies, only to find out that we had been booked into a derelict house.

'Nobody lives here,' said Liam, moaning, 'Tom set us up, the dirty bastard.'

The remnants of a once-occupied flat lay scattered around the floor of the large living room. Old clothes and papers led a path to an adjacent kitchen, which was filled with mouldy dishes and a tea cloth that was home to nasty bacterial life forms. In a corner lay a wastepaper basket covered with blood stains which extended in swirls up the wall.

'Someone's been sliced up a treat in here, Doctor Watson,' I surmised.

'We should clear off out of here. It's just our luck to get blamed for wrecking the place,' said Liam.

'Na, let's have a butcher's around first,' I replied.

We started to poke through the junk and disarray; it was similar to the abandonment of the *Mary Celeste* without the meticulous tidiness. In an old dresser in the corner, we found a discarded pair of skid-marked underpants and a few different-coloured socks. Rizla papers, or skins used for rolling tobacco, were scattered in another drawer along with some cigarette butts crammed inside a small tin.

The former residents had known how to economise; I had seen this practice before. Any civilised hobo or young budding smoker would scour the streets, collecting any unfinished cigarettes, which they would then break up for the tobacco. Then after acquiring the skins, they would roll their own smokes and puff away at what was known in the trade as roadside Virginia.

Liam had opened an envelope and begun to read a letter, while I knocked a tennis ball against a wall, using an expensive-looking squash racket.

'Hey, listen to this,' said Liam, hoping that I'd put the racket down and give his head peace from the *thump, thump* in the background. 'Somebody is in deep shite. It looks like he's knocked some girl up the duff, and now she is demanding he take responsibility and pay up,' he continued.

'I wonder who he is. Maybe we can blackmail him,' I said.

'Aye, we have to find him first. I can't read the name,' replied Liam.

Having sifted through old newspapers and sticky porn magazines, we decided there was nothing in the flat that was worth pilfering apart from the squash racket and tennis ball, which I'd taken a fancy to.

'Come on, let's get out of this dump. We've got to meet Beaker at opening time somewhere,' said Liam.

'He told us to go to the Barley Mow in London Street,' I replied.

'Aye, wherever that is, it's probably derelict too,' mumbled Liam.

Not knowing any streets in Reading and unsure about asking directions in our Belfast accents, we decided to take a stroll along the canal path and enjoy the scenery. First impressions were quite favourable as the morning sunshine reflected on the calm flow of the waterway. However, as we neared the town centre, the canal was exposed as a prime dumping ground for old bikes, mattresses, and an abundance of Reading lobster pots (shopping trolleys, Tesco's being the most popular).

Tropical part of England, my arse, I thought.

Somehow, we made our way to London Street. But it was Sunday, and the pub did not open until twelve noon, so we had half an hour to kill time. Liam sprawled out on the path for a wee snooze, while I passed the time by beating the tennis ball against the surrounding shop windows. By opening time, Beaker and Tom were already in the pub, let in early through the back door by Danny's girlfriend, the daughter of the landlord. With a short two-hour window, most places in Reading got packed pretty quickly as the bell for last orders didn't take long to come around. A few of the crowd that had been in Cherry's and the Nags Head the night before had gathered to meet in the Barley Mow. Jimmy, one of the Flower Pot brothers, greeted me as he entered the bar, but suddenly he became confrontational.

'Oy, that's my squash racket!' he exclaimed, expecting me to give it up. 'Where did you get it from?'

'Aye, dead on, it's your racket,' I answered sarcastically. 'It's mine. I found it in an old beat-up house in Baker Street, so you can clear aff.' I then pointed the racket directly at Beaker and Tom.

'Oh aye, and you two, thanks very much for setting us up in some abandoned old shite hole that someone had been carved up in,' I said angrily.

Then Liam joined in with the verbal abuse. 'Aye, that's right. Yer both a couple of slimy bastards.'

Tom seemed genuinely confused and turned to Jimmy and asked, 'Does Greg live at 40 Baker Street?'

'No, he lives at 44 Baker Street. Forty is the old flat that a few of us lived in for a while until we got flung out for not paying the rent,' replied Jimmy, still eyeing the squash racket in my hand.

'Oh no. Sorry, boys, I sent you to the wrong address,' said Tom. The others laughed at the misunderstanding.

And then I asked, 'So, who got knifed? Why was there loads of blood everywhere?'

Jimmy began sniggering as he recalled the incident. 'That mess was caused by mad Rab, but he wasn't stabbed. His foreskin got snagged in his zip and an artery in his knob exploded, squirting blood everywhere, so he grabbed the bin and bled into it.'

It was a strange but believable story. I offered the squash racket to Jimmy for the price of a pint, and then we settled down to join the others.

After the brief two hours in the Barley Mow, we enjoyed an extended intermission with some downtime at Tom's house before the pubs opened again at seven o'clock. We'd decided to go back to Cherry's Wine Bar for a second evening as things felt a bit more familiar to us by then. More of Beaker's acquaintances were introduced to Liam and me, including another Marty, also from Belfast, along with townies Jimmy and Derry Gerry. We were told that Jimmy worked for a company called DCW, otherwise known informally as Dogs, Cats, and Wankers. We met Rosie, a talented local musician who was the star in his own band and loved experimenting with mischievous pranks. Busting a blood capsule in his mouth and letting the liquid ooze down his chin was a reliable favourite. Then at last there were some women in our company, including sisters Julia and Cathy and another girl called Lorraine. Schoolteacher Julia and Beaker had had an on–off relationship for years.

When the evening ended, I somehow found myself separated from Beaker and Liam and had no idea where I was going to sleep. Thinking about the night before when we had ended up in the wrong flat, I decided to make my way to 44 rather than 40 Baker Street and have another go. On top of not having sorted out my sleeping quarters, I had foolishly agreed with Bobby that I would start work with his company the next morning.

When I arrived at the correct house, this time I banged on the door, but no one answered. At first, I thought it was another set-up, but I noticed a light was on when I looked through the letter box. I banged the door knocker louder, but there was still no answer. Once again, I was baffled. I didn't want to go back to the derelict flat two doors down as from time to time, squatters and homeless bums would use the place for shelter.

Then I decided to try to go around the back. Each of the terraced houses had an adjoining wall with the row of houses directly behind. The walls were only about four feet high, so I began climbing them at the end of Baker Street, carefully counting down the numbers and hoping that I would eventually reach the back of the right house. I was attacked by dogs, caused alley cats in the middle of shagging to scatter, and smashed various glass enclosures, all the while getting abused by anyone I had wakened up. Hurriedly, I tried the back door, but it was locked, so now I was stuck outside the rear of the house instead of the front.

I was in a bit of a panic as some anxious neighbours began flicking on porch lights and stepping outside to see who had caused all the commotion and to survey the damage. The next move had to be quick, so I tried to clamber up a drainpipe to an open second-floor window, but I slipped off and landed on my arse on top of a dustbin. I had to get into the house before I was railroaded out of town by a posse of angry locals.

I began banging the window and shouting, 'Oy, you in there, let me in!'

To my amazement, the person on the other side partially slid the window up. In an instant, I was through and on to the floor as I knocked him to one side. I lay down in the corner, dying for a sleep.

'Holy shite! Who are you? Are you mad? What do you want?' was the response from the somewhat-frightened resident. He took a defensive stance like a praying mantis as he stood over me. All I wanted

---

to do was to get my head down, but it was difficult with someone yapping in my lughole.

I half turned my body, lifted my head, and groaned, 'Are you Greg? Beaker sent me. Now leave me alone.'

'Oh, I suppose that's OK,' replied Greg to his semi-conscious intruder as he climbed back into bed, totally bemused.

The next morning, I somehow managed to wake up in time to realise I was supposed to start work with Bobby. My body had the bouquet of a docker's armpit, and my breath could have tipped over an Aberdeen Angus from a distance of ten paces. I staggered across the room and began to shake Greg, shouting into his earhole, 'Wake up, wake up! I don't know where I am!'

He was deep into the land of Nod, out for the count, which was surprising considering that a crazed person had climbed through his window in the early morning hours. I yelled again into his lugs, and then finally his eyeballs rolled open.

'Oh, are you still here? What do you want?' he asked.

'Where's the Bedford Road? I need to meet someone there,' I replied.

'What? Go down Russell Street, then you'll see the Battle Inn. That's Bedford Road. Now go away and leave me alone,' said Greg before falling back asleep.

I began walking towards Bedford Road and noticed a few beat-up old vans parked near the Battle Inn, where some people were mingling.

Bobby clocked me and shouted, *'Over here. I can't believe you turned up. You must be nuts!'*

I strolled over to join the others standing around. I asked, 'What do you want me to do?'

'Jump in that blue Ford Transit. You'll be driving a crew to Swindon,' said Bobby.

'Swindon, my ballicks. Where's that? I hardly know where Reading is,' I answered, shaking my head.

'Don't worry. The Paddies will show you how to get to the M4 then follow the signposts,' said Bobby.

The Paddies were the basis of British humour at the time, and they were portrayed as being as daft as a brush.

I sat in the driver's seat, waiting patiently for my cargo to arrive. As I looked to the right, I spotted some movement from the hedges that surrounded the Battle Inn. Two unkempt hefty gentlemen dressed in suits a couple of sizes too small for them began to crawl out and up on to their feet. These unshaven zombies approached slowly, like something out of a scene from *Dawn of the Dead*. The red-faced ogres with long bushy sideburns inched their way towards the row of vans across the street. Suddenly, these tight-suited people began to appear from everywhere and slowly filled up the parked vans like cows boarding a cattle truck. My van was soon filled and ready to hit the road.

There was a bang on the roof, then a shout: 'OK, on to Swindon!'

Not quite the size of Reading and located in Wiltshire, Swindon was a forty-mile drive west on the road to Bristol. There was nothing of note concerning this town, though Isambard Kingdom Brunel did set up the Swindon Works to do a bit of maintenance on the expanding Great Western Railway network. Unlike their neighbours, Swindon had managed to stay in the third division that year, finishing in a respectable eleventh position. They never again managed to reach the heights they hit following that remarkable league cup final against Arsenal in 1969 when Don Rogers stole the show with two fantastic extra-time goals in a 3–1 victory.

I started the van and drove around the block on to Oxford Road and felt like I was already lost as the road almost certainly went to Oxford, as the name suggested. There were no signposts for the M4, so it was down to my fine Irish friends to assist me in my pursuit of a road to Swindon. But it was too late; they were all comatose, knocking out zeds. It was hard to breathe in a van that smelt like a vat of Guinness mixed with egg-and-onion sandwiches, so I continued my search for the elusive town with my head hanging out of the window.

Ten minutes later, I was back at the Bedford Road. Rather than waste any more time, I followed another van that was headed towards the M4 until I could see the signposts for Swindon. On arrival at the building site, I had to stir my sleeping beauties to get them out the door, ready for work. The foreman approached the van to show me where it was best to park, and as I was new to the job site, I had to sign in at his office. As far as I was concerned, my job was done, and it was back to Reading for more cargo.

'There must be some mistake mate. I thought all I had to do was to drive this lot to Swindon, that's all,' I said.

'Who are you, Lord Bollocks? If someone told you that, then he was talking shit. Now get your arse in gear and start digging like the others,' said the foreman, not believing what he had just heard.

So that was it for me. I was unofficially one of the Paddies, helping in the construction of a large car park. The seasoned construction workers were thoroughly entertained watching a skinny kid from Belfast being shown how to operate a shovel correctly. I struggled along, taking excessively long periods of time to shift exceptionally small particles of gravel to different locations. During my many rest periods, I watched in amazement as my robust compatriots juggled huge paving kerbs like pebbles and laid them uniformly in place around the allotted area.

After the first week, I was a beaten docket, totally burnt out as I drove back and forth to Swindon, working full out on a building site for the first time in my life. Most of the Paddies were paid by the day, and some of them went straight into the Battle Inn after work to blow their hard-earned cash. It was not unusual to see a few of them sleeping in the streets or surrounding parks after they'd drunk themselves into oblivion, but they were always ready for work the next day. The dodgy builder whom these fine labourers worked for gave each employee the option to either start a wee bit later each Thursday or take it off completely. That was the day when everyone signed on to do the double—or working while on the dole—and I was also soon to be part of this suitable arrangement. I was a bit wary at first because getting caught doing the double in Belfast could have resulted in a penalty of up to six months in jail. That was the last thing I wanted to happen as I had just cracked the language barrier and I was beginning to enjoy the laid-back life in old Reading town.

CHAPTER 2

THE WRATH OF THE BIG GINGER

After sleeping rough for the first week, Liam and I rented a room in South Street after seeing an ad in a shop window offering accommodation to Irish men only. Strange indeed, but we were almost Irish, so why not apply? The next weekend, Liam went for a drink with his new steel-fixer workmates, so Beaker and I went to the Boars Head, a very popular and trendy pub. It was there that I saw Nancy again. We had crossed paths the previous Saturday when I was playing pool with her brother Steve in Cherry's Wine Bar. I remembered her because she and her cousin Maggie had kept grabbing my arse just as I was about to play an important shot and I was not sure if Steve had put them up to it or not.

Nancy and I exchanged familiarities with little in the way of conversation that day, but I perhaps saw a roguish trait about her that I liked. Maybe something transpired during that brief interaction, because she would later play a big part in my life. Her background was indeed interesting to say the least.

Nancy Wilson was born very young in her parents' house at 16 Jesse Terrace, Reading, on 26 May 1959 not long after Elton John's uncle Roy Dwight had scored the first goal for Nottingham Forest in the FA Cup final. It was a hard-fought 2–1 victory over Luton Town, and he was later carried off before half-time with a broken leg. As no substitutes were allowed in those days, his team had to play the rest of the game with ten men. As for Nancy, her parents had at long last a girl to go with her four older brothers: Tom, John, Stuart, and Steve. After the first three boys were born, the family decided to move from Scotland to England for a better life, not wanting the children to grow up in Third World surroundings. Nancy and her brother Steve were born in Reading. They were all, of course, quite mad. There is nothing more dangerous than Glaswegians with English accents, especially the ginger ones. As you can imagine, having four older brothers to follow Nancy was a handful growing up.

She and her ever-constant sidekick and cousin, Maggie, were inseparable and caused mayhem as they mischievously went about their business. Of course, no one would confront Nancy and Maggie because it would have meant that they had to deal with the Wilson brothers. They got away with murder (not literally); they were trouble. Their escapades were the stuff of legend. For starters, they frequently insulted people for no particular reason. One such unfortunate old man was verbally abused by the cousins; they began to shout at him, "Baldy, oh baldy!" Then they threw bricks at his greenhouse and smashed a few panes in the process before dashing off down the road, giggling. The old geezer could move, though, and he gave chase on his bicycle and caught up to the mischievous girls. They thought they were done for until he asked if they had seen two boys running by in the last few minutes. Both of them pointed instinctively and sent him in the direction of Castle Hill, and then they laughed so hard they nearly peed their pants.

A popular pastime for the pair was to bunk off school. They'd go to the River Thames, where they would check for boats before jumping off the bridge into the filthy water. On occasions, the two rapscallions—usually armed with a radio, a box of Jaffa Cakes, and a bottle of lemonade—spent perfect sunny days at the Burghfield Gravel Pits. They'd get sunburnt while listening to Minnie Ripperton, 10cc, and other bands. Once on their way home, they found time for some more window-smashing. They thought their target was a derelict house but realised that it was the home of a little old lady who was innocently asleep on her bed. This act of being ill-disciplined was a step too far and made Nancy and Maggie feel horrible. It was then that they decided to end their days of wantonly breaking glass.

One day, on an expedition exploring an area that was to be demolished to build the Butts Centre, they were to have the closest call of their naive young lives. They met a man in one of the derelict houses. He was probably twenty-five years old and very well spoken, and he said he was looking for treasure.

They were intrigued, and he threw them even better bait. 'I find all kinds of treasures in old houses, but it's usually up in the loft because people moving out in a hurry forget to empty the loft.' Their imaginations were racing when he said, 'I'm going to see what's up in the loft. Would you like to come up there with me? Anything we find we can share.'

They were young, gullible, stupid, and most certainly never listened to all the warnings and sound advice that their mums had dished out on a daily basis. He lifted Maggie up into the loft. Next, when he was lifting Nancy, a man's stern voice was heard.

'Get them down,' he said.

It was a security guard with a large dog. They were all taken to a portable office, where the guard called the police.

The girls thought, *Why is this bad man being rude to our new friend?*

Nancy and Maggie gave a show of solidarity with Loft Man by sharing their sweets with him but deliberately not offering any to the security guard. Eventually, their mums came to get them, and although they were very angry, they hugged their daughters so hard that the girls could barely breathe. Nancy and Maggie didn't know what all the fuss was about until a policewoman came to Nancy's house and told her that the man was a registered sex offender. That security guard had saved them from a possible sexual assault or maybe even worse. They learned a valuable lesson that day.

Of course, a leopard never changes its spots. The girls would regularly go scrumping in the orchard at the Lima in Bath Road. This area was once a nunnery that backed on to Nancy's house in Jesse Terrace. After a previous raid, the two girls had thrown the stolen fruit from the top window of Nancy's house and knocked a man off his moped. Unfortunately for them, he saw the direction the missiles had come from. After dusting himself down, he marched to the front door to advise Nancy's mum that people on the street were under attack by two top-floor apple-wielding waifs. Nancy ended up with a skelped arse as did Maggie when she got home. Nancy's mum was particularly pissed off because she had been watching the Wednesday night Hollywood musical downstairs and trying to have a bit of peace after a hard day on the line at Huntley and Palmers.

By the time Nancy had reached eighteen, she was a hardened, streetwise, pint-swigging teen. One night, as she assisted an inebriated friend along the road to where he lived, some wise guy began to bother her and tried to get lucky. The unsuspecting clown would not take no for an answer and made a move, touching her bum in the process. That was a big mistake. Like a true Wilson, she clocked her assailant with a firm right hook, laying him out with a suspected busted nose. Her friend grunted, oblivious to what was occurring, and was helped on his way by the girl who would later be known as Scrapper Wilson. Was anyone mad enough to get involved with such a dangerous girl? Surely not! What kind of family did she come from?

Her mother, Ena, was everything that her father, Willie, was not. She was kind, caring, and full of life. Willie, on the other hand, could be a nasty piece of work. He had spent nine months incarcerated in Glasgow's notorious prison, Barlinnie, locally known as Bar L, for slapping people about and breaking into shops. His aggression did not wane much once he was south of the border, and he was lucky to avoid a stretch in Reading Jail. A few months before Nancy was born, Willie purchased a car from a local gypsy who was a known shady dealer. Willie had become infuriated when the old banger rarely started, so he demanded a refund. His anger increased when he was told to take a hike by the arrogant seller, and when a second request for reimbursement was ignored, Willie lost the plot. He went to the office alone one evening to confront the person who had sold him the car. The dealership owners were a family of tough-nut occasional criminals and were well known in the local underworld. They could be quite intimidating and usually had a couple of snarling Alsatians by their sides. These wild hounds were left in the yard at night to guard the premises.

The geezer whom Willie was interested in was there on his own this particular night, but before Willie could approach him, he would have to negotiate his way past the vicious dogs. Willie came prepared with a few lumps of meat laced with enough sedatives to knock the poor mutts out for an hour or so. When this first part of the plan was in place, Willie deftly made his way to the display cars parked along the perimeter and poured sugar into the petrol tanks. Then he strolled over to the office and casually kicked the door in. Before the dealer had any idea of what was occurring, Willie was on top of him. He then proceeded to punch his target's lights out with a small Schweppes bottle that he had inserted into the palm of his hand. This old Glasgow trick created a solid fist with the effect of being punched by an iron bar. The result was devastating. Willie had beaten his adversary to a pulp and rendered him unconscious. It wouldn't be long before Willie was apprehended and charged with GBH.

This left Ena quite concerned about how she would be able to raise a new baby and four young sons if her husband was to be jailed.

Expecting the worst, Ena's mother, Peggy, and her younger brother Jim moved down from Glasgow for moral support. Although he could have been handed a lengthy jail term, the case was thrown out of court when Willie convinced the judge that he was mentally unstable. It wasn't far from the truth though; Willie was definitely nuts. The judge agreed that Willie was in need of some treatment and ordered that he should spend some time at the Fairmile Mental Institution. So in order to avoid a couple of years in the clink, Willie had to endure three months of being prodded and examined by strange doctors in white coats. This left Ena in a complicated situation as not only did she have to keep the kids from running wild, she also had to deal with the stigma of her husband being a raving loony.

It would not be the only time in his life that Willie would get one up on the authorities. Although he was to mellow somewhat in later years, he would always have a malicious way about him.

So why was I so drawn to Nancy, this potential femme fatale, not to mention her unstable family? Maybe it was because the Wilsons reminded me of certain Belfast families with their unpredictable demeanour. There was also an Irish connection. Willie's father, Tug, was born in Ballymena, County Antrim, and Ena's grandfather Tommy Baxter lived in Belfast and helped to build the *Titanic*. The Wilson side of the family certainly had a colourful history. Before arriving in Scotland, a couple of their ancestors had had a fine old time while residing on the holy island of Lindisfarne in Northumberland off the northeast coast of England. Nancy's great-great-grandmother Annie Stamp and her sister Christian Stamp were renowned ladies of the night and plied their trade in or around the Crown and Anchor Pub. They lived at the adjoining and aptly named cottages, the Crofts. The island was lightly populated, and everyone knew the Stamp sisters, which made them celebrities in their own right. They made a decent income selling their bodies to local punters and visitors to the sacred isle who were keen to spend some time with the girls of ill repute.

But enough about ancient history. Back to the Boars Head, where an event of great significance was about to take place. At closing time, Beaker asked me if I fancied a drive to London to see an ex-girlfriend of his so they could catch up on old times. His primary objective though was to try to get a leg over. It was not the best idea in the world as we'd both had a few pints, but when Nancy asked if she could go with us, my mind was made up. With the help of my previous knowledge of the London area and a lot of luck, I negotiated the myriad of one-way streets, though not always in the right direction. Beaker informed me that the girl we would be staying with was called Adrian—a strange name for a girl indeed—and that I would really like her.

We banged on the door, but rather than welcoming us with open arms, Adrian seemed quite surprised to find the three of us on the doorstep. Either Beaker hadn't told her in advance that we would be paying a visit or she had a problem with short-term memory. Beaker introduced me to Adrian, whom Nancy had met before, and she invited us in after coming to terms with the fact that we would be staying overnight. Nancy and I really got to know each other that night and seemed comfortably at ease as we talked about any old shit into the morning hours. It felt like we'd known each other for years.

The next day, Beaker had arranged to meet two mates—also from Northern Ireland—at the Swiss Cottage Pub in St John's Wood. The pub was a typical old English gem with large wooden ceiling beams and low doorways designed to crack the skull of anyone over five foot four each time they came in or went for a piss. After a much-needed urination session, I came back from the toilet.

Rubbing my head, I asked Beaker, 'Who are we meeting, and where are they from?'

'Eugene and Jimmy, otherwise known as Jimmy Kilkeel,' he replied.

Using my superior powers of deduction, I concluded that they were probably from Kilkeel, a small fishing town in County Down that I'd been to a couple of times. Nancy already knew the pair, along with most of Beaker's friends, through her brother Steve. About fifteen minutes later, the lads, whose names both suspiciously started with *Mc*, arrived.

'Here they are now,' said Beaker.

Jimmy entered first, and then Eugene followed, banging his nut on the door frame. Beaker introduced the pair to me, and my first impressions were that Eugene looked like an Italian and Jimmy looked like Eugene's da. Jimmy was in fact a bearded fisherman type and not Eugene's father at all. We all got on well, and Eugene told me that he had gone to Felden, the same government training centre that I had attended. He had left the year I had started, so we nearly knew each other already. After a couple of pints each, we all headed back to Adrian's house for the night just to annoy her for a while longer.

On the following Saturday, in Cherry's Wine Bar, I was faced with an incendiary situation that could easily have led to my very painful demise. Beaker and Liam were already in the pub, and I turned up a little later. On arrival, I nodded to them as they sat at a corner table with a couple of others; one of them, I assumed, was Nancy's brother Steve. As I ordered a drink at the bar, the tall ginger rose from the table and approached. But as he got closer, I realised it wasn't Steve, though it certainly looked like him. I knew Steve had three older brothers, and this muscular bastard was certainly one of them, probably Tom. He strutted over to me like John Wayne. Tom was the oldest, sort of like the godfather, and I'd heard he was as hard as nails and that if you crossed him, you were toast. There were stories of grown men tearing their own throats out rather than confronting Tom.

He stood next to me and said, 'Are you Crofty?'

Uh-oh, I thought. *What does he want with me?*

Nervously I prepared myself, thinking I should deny it, but I answered, 'Yes.'

He glared right into my eyes and asked, 'Did you shag my sister?'

My mind started racing at 100 miles per hour as I looked around for an escape route, all the while thinking about the other two brothers and that they must be here as well. So that was it. I was done for.

'N-n-no, you must have mixed me up with somebody else,' I replied with my heart beating as fast as a Speedy Gonzales's fart after a spicy burrito. I placed my pint on the bar, and just as I was about to start hurdling customers to do a runner, he placed his hand on my shoulder.

He said, 'Don't worry, mate. There's no problem. Nancy set you up.'

With my knees rattling, I grabbed a pint—any pint—and sunk it in one go. *Nice one, Nancy,* I thought. *Why would she do this evil thing to a person as nice as me?*

She was a handful, no question. One evening, she inadvertently put me in hospital on our way to the Target, a popular bar that had some good musical acts on show. For reasons unknown to neither man nor wildebeest, this place was built below ground level. It was accessible only by a steep staircase which led there from an enclosed doorway situated just behind the Butts Centre. It was a disaster waiting to happen. Almost everyone smoked then, so a carelessly discarded cigarette could easily have resulted in an underground inferno, but no one seemed to be concerned about the probability of such a trivial catastrophe occurring.

For the second week in a row, an all-girl punk band was playing. The Cunning Stunts had played the week before, and although there hadn't been any tickets available that night, we were lucky enough to get some to see the Slits in action. It was beneficial to be downstairs early to get a spot close to the stage, so we were well ahead of schedule in preparation for a good night.

A few of the others walked up to the main doors on this beautiful summer's night, and I strolled just behind, whistling away with my hands in my pockets and not a care in the world. Then within seconds, the lights went out! My next recollection was of being face down in the gutter with blood pumping from my forehead as I sniffed the roadside. Had I been hit by a brick?

I was semiconscious, and my head was throbbing like a busted trombone. But I had no idea what had happened! Nancy was the first to rush to my aid, which made me feel that she was really a caring person and not an impish rogue after all. Then I found out why I was writhing in agony with my brains knocked in. Little elfin Nancy had bounded across the road and leaped on to my back, sending me crashing to the ground like a great redwood. Her uninvited piggyback had resulted in a nosedive on to the kerb, which had cracked my skull open.

She did accompany me to the Battle Hospital though, where she witnessed an extremely ugly nurse insert ten stitches into my open wound. The kindly nurse did not hold back skewering her way through my skin and was unconcerned about my agonised cries for mercy. Things might have been different had I not foolishly commented on her grotesque features just as she was threading the needle.

CHAPTER 3

THE TURKEY AND THE ELUSIVE MOUSE

My old mate Michael arrived in August, and it didn't take long before I ended up in the same hospital that Nancy had put me in a few weeks earlier. On his first night in Reading, we had a session in Cherry's, and then after the pub closed, he was immediately up for some tomfoolery. He thought it would be a good idea to climb on to the top of a building to try to break in or maybe just abuse passers-by on the street below. He was on a mission, and as quick as a flash, Michael shimmied his way up a tree and swung across a branch like a sloshed gibbon as he made his way on to the roof.

Like an idiot, I went up as well, and the last thing I remember was the sound of the branch snapping. I then free-fell on to a concrete path below, where I landed safely on my head. I'd been knocked out cold, and an ambulance was summoned. The next morning, I wakened in a hospital bed with my high hair caked in blood and a severe headache. I eased myself out of the bed to see exactly where I was, but nothing seemed familiar about the place. My clothes were on a chair at the bedside, so I dressed myself and wandered down the hallway to the nurse's station.

The friendly lady on duty asked me why I was walking around and suggested that I should return to bed as I'd suffered a serious head injury.

'I'm OK. Show me the way out,' I murmured.

'You can't leave without signing yourself out, but you should talk to a doctor first,' she replied, somewhat concerned.

'Aye, maybe. Where's the paperwork?' I groaned.

Apprehensively she placed the sign-out sheet in front of me, and I scrawled down my name then left. As I stood outside on the main street, shivers ran through me, and although it was a warm day, I felt very cold. A bus destined for the train station approached, and I boarded it, rifling through my pockets and scrambling to find enough change to make the fare. I sat on the top deck, and my head pounded as the bus stopped and started in time with each ring of the bell.

As I gazed out of the window from the front seat I became really confused. *When did they repaint all of the buses?* I thought. *Could they have possibly changed the fleet's bright-red colouring to maroon overnight?*

Something was not right. None of the streets or shops looked familiar, nor did the hospital that I'd just left. And most puzzling of all was that everyone spoke with an English accent. The unusual state of affairs seemed to compound my head-pain as I struggled to comprehend what was happening to me. During the bus ride, I stared at each building with an empty feeling that knotted my gut. Nothing was the same; I felt like I was going mad. When we finally arrived at the train station, I disembarked and stood motionless on the pavement, cupping my hands over my ears as I tried to soften the harsh traffic sounds that buzzed inside my skull. I turned full circle as I attempted to get to grips with the tricks that my mind was playing on me.

Then the penny dropped. The large Reading sign on display at the main entranceway of the train station jump-started my brain. Slowly it began to click. The blow to the head had really done a number on me. Up until that point, I had believed that I was still in Belfast and not Reading. The foggy haze lifted as I had entered the town centre, and as Cherry's Wine Bar was just a stone's throw away, I did what anyone would do after cracking their skull open: I went for a pint. The usual crowd was there, and after the initial surprise of my unexpected appearance wore off, they nodded to each other and carried on drinking.

Later, a girl whom I had been out with once before—affectionately known as the Rabbit—became concerned when I began slurring and talking shit. I'm sure that if she had known me a bit longer, it would not have been an issue as she would have thought it was just business as usual. But she was genuinely worried that I was in trouble and suggested that I go home and rest or at least get cleaned up. My hair was still matted with particles of flesh, and my blue T-shirt was liberally sprinkled with blood spatter. Reluctantly, I downed my last pint and walked back to my digs in South Street with her. As I approached the front doorway, my legs began to buckle, and the Rabbit had to support me from falling over.

'I'm all right. Let me go on myself,' I mumbled before collapsing like a sack of spuds at her feet.

Cue another ambulance. This time, the hospital police made sure that I did not do a runner, and I was detained for one week as various brain surgeons from exotic parts of the world observed my progress. I had sustained a heavy concussion. Julia visited me during my stay, and her sister Cathy kindly turned up every day and supplied some fine fruity delights, which helped lift my spirits. Although I was deeply stitched up and had a pounding headache, it was the best accommodation in Reading I'd had to date.

Even though Michael was a complete balloon, he did get us some sort of long-term stability when he managed to snag a two-bedroom flat in the busy Southampton Street. It also meant that I had somewhere to park the company vehicle instead of sleeping in it! Location, they say, is everything, and the flat was perfectly situated amongst an array of delightful little taverns—a dreamland for the sophisticated youth of that time.

If you fell fast enough down the stairway and out of the front door, you could roll right across the street and into the Cambridge Arms or possibly the close-by Hop Leaf. Within a five-minute stroll down Southampton Street, you could wet your whistle in the Crown, the Red Cow, and the Red Lion. Walking another few minutes in the opposite direction would take you to the Greyhound, the Woodley Arms, and the Wellington. And if you fancied a longer ten-minute stroll, then the Barley Mow and the Turk's Head awaited.

The flat was on the top floor of a large house; it included a bathroom, a kitchen, two single beds in one room, and a single in the other. The front entrance was shared with the flat below. Michael and I drew the short straws and ended up sharing the room with two beds, while Liam got the other one. Beaker stayed periodically, still preferring to sleep around. While I was digging holes for a living, Michael had used his smart-bastard skills to gain employment as an accountant with Coopers and Lybrand in the Reading town centre. Beaker had used his not-so-smart-bastard skills to maintain his position as part of the clean-up crew which was making the grounds of the newly completed Hexagon Theatre look presentable. Michael was well educated with three A levels, and although he hadn't gone to university, he'd paid his own way through college so that he could gain his accountancy licence. The old saying of 'Never judge a book by its cover' was based on Michael. He spoke and dressed well and was very polite but was in fact a mental case.

Not long after moving into our new flat, the two of us went to the Red Cow just across the street to celebrate having our own place. Michael was very unpredictable. I'd gone to the toilet and returned to the table where we had been sitting just in time to see him leaving the pub. He began walking towards the busy intersection of London Road and London Street. I followed, making sure that he did not know I was behind him as I had a feeling that he was about to do something unconventional. He climbed on to the top of a postbox and sat with legs crossed like a constipated gargoyle and began to make obscene gestures at passing motorists. It looked quite entertaining, so I headed up to the crossroads and joined in with the uncalled verbal abuse of innocent Sunday drivers, some of them perhaps on their way to church. Michael scrambled down when a gleaming black limousine complete with uniformed driver pulled up to the red stop light.

With a roguish twinkle in his eye he said to me, 'C'mon, let's get in.'

I instantly followed my pal's lead as he opened the Daimler's back door and said, 'After you, my good man.'

We entered and slouched back into the comfy leather seats, and then Michael addressed the chauffeur: 'Onwards, my good man. Take us to the ball.'

The enraged driver glanced over his shoulder in disbelief and began yelling, 'Get out of the car! Get out of the car!'

We never budged and began pointing in the forward direction, chanting 'Onward! Onward!' and occasionally giving the Queen's wave to curious bystanders. The driver was becoming more and more infuriated, so he jumped out of the car and opened the back door in an effort to evict his unwanted passengers. As he grabbed at us, we sidled across the seat and jumped out the opposite door, waving our arms in the air and inviting him to confront us. The now extremely incensed man dashed to the other side of the car in futile pursuit as we raced back round to where we started. This time Michael locked the doors once inside, leaving the poor red-faced driver helpless on the roadside as we watched him throw his cap on to the ground. It was evident that this man was close to exploding as he tugged at the door handle in despair.

As we watched the pitiful driver go into a meltdown, Michael nonchalantly turned to me and said, 'Back to the pub?'

'Aye, let's blow,' I replied.

We shifted over to the door away from our adversary then jumped from the car and began running down London Street as fast as we could move. In a final defying insult, we turned to thrust two fingers up, singing 'Wanker, wanker!' as we sped off, laughing hysterically. The forlorn chauffeur climbed back into his Daimler in an effort to complete his rudely interrupted assignment. The abuse wasn't quite over for him as he attempted to appease the irate motorists who had been caught up in the traffic jam behind him, blaring their horns.

Michael loved Cherry's Wine Bar and would often go there during his lunch break for a sandwich and a quick six pints of lager. Tony, the landlord, thought it was great having us there in the early days, but eventually we drove him mental by taking advantage of his softness. Our impish pursuits included nicking display wines off the bar and replacing them with bottles we'd earlier filled with water. Our clever ploy was to distract him with the old 'Look behind you, Tony!' routine, but we taught him a valuable lesson as he soon began to use water-filled bottles for his displays.

We'd have arguments about the size of the measurement and mixtures added to vodka and other tipples. I had a difference of opinion with him when I asked for a vodka and white (white lemonade). He laughed at me because to him lemonade was indeed white and he wondered why I was informing him of its colour. I went into a rant about his lack of knowledge of soft drinks, explaining to him that there were two types of lemonade: brown and white. It was a sad state of affairs as the unfortunate people of Reading had only one colour of lemonade available in their fine country. Michael then accused him of not putting enough vodka in his glass. We later found out that everyone was getting ripped off as the measures in England were smaller than they were in Belfast but cost the same.

Michael, in particular, sent Tony twitching nervously when in his presence. He was a timid wee man and had trouble getting people to leave at closing time.

When everyone totally ignored him, he would walk around the bar, wagging his finger and clucking, 'Come now. Please leave. It's a pub, not a club—a pub, not a club.'

Michael would follow in his shadow, mimicking his voice and actions right down to the finger-wagging. It was all innocent fun and just a coincidence that Tony died a babbling idiot.

A particular problem we had in Reading at that time was our accents. None of the English people had a clue what we were saying, especially when I spoke; it would have been easier if we'd spoken German. According to Nancy, she did not realise that I had been asking her out for two weeks. Apparently, we talked too quickly, but I think it was a feeble excuse; it was quite obvious to me that they just didn't listen fast enough. Eventually, most people tuned into our bastardised English as we got to know the locals.

One fine Englishman was so laid back that he didn't care what we were saying. Pill Head was an eccentric gangly human being similar to the character played by John Hurt in *Midnight Express* and was well known in the area for supplying some illicit home-grown needs. He certainly grabbed our attention with stories of his collection of grass plants which were strategically placed in an assortment of flower beds throughout the town centre. These plants were carefully cultivated along with the beautiful floral arrangements by the horticultural branch of Reading Borough Council, which was totally unaware that it was aiding in illegal activities. Pill Head described how he waited until the time was right to harvest the grass then baked it at home in his oven until it was ready to be sold off for a nice profit.

I was quite naive as far as drugs were concerned, and although I knew what cannabis was, I was thinking that Pill Head was talking about selling everyday lawn grass. I imagined Pill Head had some magical way of transforming the abundant lush turf into something potent and ready for smoking, and I was keen to get involved in this simple but brilliant money-making scheme. Pill Head invited us back to his house when the pub closed, and I was rubbing my hands in expectation of making a lot of cash from very little work—the perfect job! On the way to his home, we stopped in the town centre at the large statue of Queen Victoria in the middle of the roundabout outside the train station, where Pill Head pointed out his prized asset. There in plain view, unbeknownst to the thousands of travellers who passed by the statue on their way in and out of the train station, was a delightful four-foot grass plant, ready to be claimed.

'I'll pick that one up tonight,' said Pill Head as he gazed in admiration at his handiwork.

I later discovered that there was a little more required to become a casual drug dealer than picking up a few grass seeds from the garden centre and planting them all over Reading. Pill Head invited us over to his place, where he showed off his array of plants, which were sporadically placed throughout the back garden along with his geraniums and daffodils. He explained the procedure of purchasing the buds and harvesting the plants for their leaves, which he then dried out and bagged so that they were ready for selling. Maybe it was a bit too much for us to comprehend, though we thoroughly enjoyed the cannabis crop rotation lesson.

Finally, the big event came to town, the Reading Music Festival, which was in full swing, and it brought with it all sorts of strange creatures to the area. Hippies in Afghan coats wandered the streets with their portable cassette radios, singing along to 'Stairway to Heaven'. Leather-clad heavy metal headbangers shook their shoulders violently as they listened to 'Smoke on the Water' and sprayed all sorts of foreign bodies out from their greasy long hair. It was like a carnival, and we loved it. The Troubles had starved us of musical acts for years as not many bands had been brave enough to take on the challenge. The relaxed atmosphere of the festival made it feel so different. Thanks to the peaceful feeling in the air, we weren't constantly expecting to be attacked by some lunatic just because we had looked at him for too long. The headliners at the festival included Uriah Heap, Golden Earring, Aerosmith, Thin Lizzy, the Doobie Brothers, Frankie Miller, and the Sensational Alex Harvey Band.

Our flat in Southampton Street became a good gathering place for anyone that had planned to go to the festival. We had become friends with Greg and his townie Derry Gerry (the same Greg whose room I had unceremoniously gate-crashed not too long before). We planned to meet Eugene and Jimmy Kilkeel at the flat when they arrived from London, then we would all head to the festival site on the banks of the River Thames. My complete wardrobe consisted of a pair of jeans and a couple of T-shirts that I also wore to work and washed at the weekends. The Derry men, on the other hand, dressed in expensive attire. Gerry was like an advert for a Marks & Spencer catalogue with his black drainpipe trousers, white leather box jacket, and various red accessories draped about his person. By the time the two London boys arrived, wearing their fine leathers, I felt like a hobo. Eugene had just picked up a new pair of expensive cowboy boots, which were all the rage back then, so he slung his old pair in the bin. Gerry started moaning that he needed new boots as well, even though the pair he was wearing looked brand new. Apparently, Greg was supposed to pick up pre-ordered new boots for Gerry, but he'd forgotten. It wasn't long before a yapping match started between the two of them. They were like a couple of old women. All those boys seemed to be financially sound as the building trade in Reading was booming at that time.

At last we were ready to get on down and boogie, but with a big fat nimbus cloud about to burst overhead, it looked like we'd be singing and dancing in the rain. Just as we walked on to Southampton Street, I sneaked back up to the flat and grabbed Eugene's old boots from the bin and dumped my smelly shoes in their place. Now I was one of the lads, even though the boots were second hand and a size too big and—as the Flower Pot Men said—they would flop a lot. Friday night at the festival was brilliant, with Thin Lizzy finishing the evening off in style by blasting out 'Whiskey in the Jar' to the delight of the massive crowd. We dragged ourselves back to Southampton Street and crashed out, completely soaked through but content. Saturday was not such a good day. The rain had not stopped, and the site was a mudbath. So we sought shelter in the nearby Moderation Pub.

As mentioned before, Michael was unpredictable, and it was not uncommon for him to just walk away from the company he was in. I was aware of this and tried to keep an eyeball on him at all times. On this occasion, I was too late to prevent him from doing the unexpected. He walked past us with a pint in his hand, mumbling about something. The rest of us were distracted by a drinking contest between Eugene and me; the two of us were attempting to find out who could gulp down a pint of water in record time. I emerged as the victor, but alas, I was never paid the five pounds, not to mention the ten pounds he already owed me from a previous bet when he guessed how old I was.

Looking around, I could see that Michael had strolled out on to the adjacent street and was walking towards Caversham Road. He seemed to be upset about something, and we watched him nonchalantly sling his empty pint mug up into the air over his shoulder. The glass smashed against a wall behind him. During the weekend of the festival, special constables were recruited to handle the sudden population increase, and as can be expected, most of these wannabe police officers were spotty, snot-faced megalomaniacs.

Unfortunately for Michael, two of these clowns had just turned the corner and caught him in the act of discarding his empty drinking apparatus in a decidedly inappropriate manner. Immediately the thugs jumped Michael and started pounding him until he hit the ground.

Then they put the boot in as he lay there. The episode happened really quickly, but not as fast as it took me to sprint out of the pub and jump on to one of the storm troopers' backs. We both crashed to the pavement, but before I could do any damage, a squad car with some real police officers arrived and lifted us both. The others in the pub could only look on in amazement at the events that had transpired so swiftly in front of their eyes. Once again Michael and I found ourselves incarcerated by Her Majesty's finest, though this time it was in the relative comfort of the Thames Valley Police Force. Each cell was furnished with a comfy blue mattress as opposed to the cold slab of wood which was standard in Belfast jails.

Before we were taken down to be shown our sleeping arrangements, Michael went around the large office area, asking each person involved in the arrest how much they earned. After calculating their combined wages, he then made a speech to anyone prepared to listen about just how much government money had been wasted in the process of booking us. I'd already begun my walk of shame towards the cells when Michael was dragged out of the offices by two police gorillas, still prattling out monetary figures as he was bundled away.

The end result was a day in court, with Michael receiving a ten-quid fine and me—the person who had sprung to his aid—receiving a twenty-quid fine. Although it was a lot of money for me to pay, I was lucky that the charge had been reduced to obstructing the police, down from the original charge of assaulting the police. That charge would have had the potential of big, big trouble for me.

During the trial, I had had no chance of pleading my case or asking for mercy from the authorities as the grumpy old female judge was not interested in my plight.

At one point she turned to her colleagues on the completion of my oration and enquired, 'What did the young boy say?' She then banged her gavel. 'Next!'

The old hag had no idea what I was on about, so she just fined me then, like clockwork, moved on to the next poor bastard. They wanted me to pay it all within a month, which I was not able to do, but Michael's trusty cheque book came to the rescue. I was in no rush to pay him back as I thought he was loaded. The last night of the festival was a much quieter affair as we enjoyed the Sensational Alex Harvey Band, who closed the event by walking on to the stage with a burning cross.

Meanwhile, I was still slaving away at the building site on weekdays. I was not too displeased when I was given the heave-ho by my distinguished employers. It had been obvious that my time was limited as I was without doubt the laziest, scrawniest, most useless hole-digger in the company's history. My termination was finalised one Saturday evening after I'd picked up Beaker and some crazy that he had been working with. We left the pub and drove down to the train station to pick up a kebab from one of the many vans parked there. While Beaker and I waited in the vehicle, his bin-head friend got into a bit of a ruckus with a few drunken patrons who were also waiting in line for a kebab. He eventually climbed in and shut the door, still shooting his mouth off, but before I could drive away, one of the lunatics came running at the van with an iron bar and sent it crashing through the passenger side window. Just as he lifted it for a second swing, I roared off, sending glass particles into the night.

I got to the end of the street and yelled at Beaker that he should sling his dickhead companion out of the van. It was obvious that Belfast did not hold the exclusive rights to fruit-and-nut cases. The next day, I left the van off at the builder's yard, knowing that my services would no longer be required, and cleared off out of it before I had to pay retribution for the smashed window. Usually, when you lose your job, the dole queue awaits, but as I was already on the dole, it meant I could now legally collect my money. My days of doing the double were over.

Liam was cheesed off with the way of life in Reading, so one fine morning, he was up on his toes and waltzed back to sunny Belfast. Now we had a spare room to rent, so the obvious choice would have been to let Beaker move in as he was living like a gypsy around various houses. It was no surprise when Liam went back, but not long after, Beaker decided that he also was ready to return home. He was missing Janet, a girl that he'd been seeing just before we left for Reading, so now his old heartstrings were twanging. It was probably for the better that Beaker did not move in permanently. During his last week, we were ready to string him up as he kept us awake each night while he recited all the lyrics of every song that Bob Dylan had ever written. So that was it. Michael and I were on our own after Beaker had pleaded with us to join him on the great adventure to the tropical paradise that was Reading.

Finding a new roommate was not going to be easy, and although we'd got to know a lot of people in such a short time, Michael and I had a reputation amongst our new associates as being not right in the head. Then out of the blue, one mug stepped forward. Greg had volunteered to enter the unknown on the condition that he got the single room. We agreed and prepared for his arrival as we set up a very unlikely triumvirate. Michael and I liked to give people personal nicknames, and Greg helped our cause one morning when he crawled out of bed with a peculiar arrangement of hair sticking up from his crust. Because of this fowl-like tuft, he would then be known as the Turkey.

Having the Turkey living with us was great as he had a 1974 Ford Escort, perfect for lifts to country pubs and other venues, such as the launderette. Even my modest collection of glad rags got heavy on the long walk to the cleaners, but with Greg and his car, it would surely be plain sailing. On one such trip, after the completion of the wash cycle, we loaded our wet items into separate dryers as Greg bragged about his collection of designer golf shirts and underwear. Rather than staring at the spinning machines, we went over to the Borough Arms for a pint. As we relaxed and talked shite, the soothing piped music of Perry Como was snuffed out by the loud wailing of a fire engine, which illuminated the night sky with its emergency lights as it roared towards us.

'Oy, look! They're going into the laundrette,' said Greg as we watched from the large window of the pub lounge.

'Aye, yer right, let's go over to see what's happened,' I replied.

We paid up and headed across the street to where a small crowd of curious spectators had gathered. The fire crew held us back until the minor fire inside the launderette had been extinguished.

'What caused the fire?' Greg asked one of the firemen.

'We think one of the dryers was overloaded,' he answered.

After a while, we were allowed to enter the premises and walked apprehensively over to the still-smoking dryer. It was Greg's. With snotters tripping me, I cracked up laughing at the look of unease on his face. He opened the lid and, with a finger and thumb, lifted out the smouldering remnants of his designer clothes, while I removed my unspoiled Woolworths underpants and stringed vests from the unblemished adjacent dryer.

With Greg living in Southampton Street, it meant we would see a lot more of Derry Gerry and his weird antics. He was one of the original air guitar players who couldn't sing a note, but that didn't stop him from jumping around the room like an eejit and abusing our eardrums. Greg would usually join in and do his version of the Sex Pistol's 'Pretty Vacant'. Eugene and Jimmy Kilkeel stayed with us at the weekends when they came up from London, so the craic was good. Jimmy fancied himself as a cook and enjoyed stuffing everything from the cupboards into a big pot to make some kind of stew, which was fine until the day he lobbed my pig's foot in. He got banned from the kitchen; no one messes with my pigs' feet. We all got on well and shared most things, but that was to soon change. Greg had been missing in action for a while, and we later found out why: he was seeing a bit of stuff. We knew this because he began to wash more often and lock his room at night; then one morning he was spotted ushering a pretty petite blonde out the front door. We assumed she was a female, but why would he not introduce her to us? There was no chance of Michael or me stealing her away from him, so perhaps he thought we were a bit too mental to meet her. The very thought of it. We later found out that she was indeed a girl and her name was Julia, but as she sneaked in and out without a word, she was to be known to us as the Mouse.

The more Greg kept her away from us, the more we wanted to meet her. But he always locked the door after skulking in with the little mousy. One Friday night before they returned home, we took the door off its hinges and hid it, leaving a wide-open entranceway to his room. The next morning, we thought that we would simply stroll in and introduce ourselves. It was a good strategy indeed but not at all foolproof. Greg had been one step ahead and had moved the wardrobe, chest of drawers, and bed against the doorway in order to prevent us from gaining entrance. Plan B was a course of action that we had not intended to use, but desperate measures were called for to resolve this war of attrition. The following Saturday, we took up the challenge by tying the door handle to the banister; then we headed off to the pub. By three in the afternoon, Greg had cracked. The need to use the toilet was too much for the entrapped lovebirds, so he agreed that we should at last meet the elusive wee Mouse. Julia was a charming little thing—though she was still shit scared of us—so we promised not to lock them in the room any more.

The inconvenience of having to pay rent meant that I had to try to get a job as Michael was getting into debt by bouncing cheques left, right, and centre. I managed to get a start in Ideal Casements, a large factory that built bus shelters and other fine metallic enclosures. Not long after starting, I contemplated resigning from my position as an essential cog in the production line when two tragic incidents occurred that rocked the music industry. On 17 August, Elvis Presley died, presumably halfway through a Big Mac; then in September, Marc Bolan departed to the great gig in the sky. Unfortunately, his last hit was a tree when he was fatally injured while travelling in the passenger seat of a car. It was not a good time for the T. Rex lead singer to clock out as his death went virtually unnoticed because everyone was still mourning the burger king. I began to wonder if these twin tragedies were somehow connected to my newfound position at Ideal Casements. Who knew who would bite the dust next if I didn't quit? I hated it, but I needed the dough. So there was no option but to hang in there and hope no one else died.

The factory was a dump; it was hot and sticky in the summer, and by October, I only got to see daylight at the weekends. It was dark on my way to work and dark when I was returning home. I had to find another job or an alternative way of making some more money before I went crazy. This became even more essential after I suddenly became £50 worse off when Michael decided to purchase a 1965 Ford Anglia between us without mentioning to me that I'd be half owner. As with everything else, Michael said that I could pay him later. He loved the old car and said that the wheels wobbling in an eccentric pattern rather than the standard circular rotation was part of its charm. On our first trip outside Reading near Maidenhead, one of the front wheels came off and shot up into the air then bounced down a hill through a hedge and into a farmer's field. When I suggested that we should get a mechanic to inspect the car, Michael insisted that swerving to avoid a hedgehog had caused the malfunction and argued that if we didn't exceed fifty miles per hour in the future, then we'd be all right.

CHAPTER 4

THE BURNING ANGLIA

Another Saturday night was upon us, and the thrill of cruising around in the Anglia, visiting different pubs, was just splendid. We met in the Butler, a place mostly frequented by hippies and the only pub in town without a jukebox. Michael had got to know Don, one of the bar staff, during his two-hour lunch breaks and had managed to get us invited to a party at his large house in Caversham. There were few people at the party that we knew, so we headed into the kitchen and helped ourselves to whatever beer and food there was in the fridge. The music was pure organic shite, and most of the clientele were stoned as they sloped around and greeted each other while rattling their beads and comparing Afghan coats.

One joker requested that the record be changed in the typical hippie fashion. 'Hey, man, have you got "Southern Man", man? Could you play it, man?'

Others rambled on about the amazing effects they were having from the finest marijuana in town. It was a load of old bollocks, and I was bored stiff and way out of my comfort zone. I was busting for a lash, but the place was bunged. The toilet was permanently occupied, so it was outside to the garden for me. What a relief! I was leaning against the wall of the house, whistling a merry tune and urinating like Red Rum, when something interesting caught my attention. Along the back fence stood a delightful row of four-foot-high grass plants arranged in perfect symmetry. Immediately, my mind recalled Pill Head and the plants he had scattered throughout the town and how he cultivated them to make a nice profit. Here right in front of me were probably ten times as many fully grown plants, which must have been worth a fortune.

I ran back into the house, found Michael, and then whispered into his ear, 'Get the Anglia.'

'What for?' he said, looking at me as if I was mad. 'It's only about half nine.'

'Just get the Anglia and reverse it up to the fence in the back garden,' I said, breathing heavily.

'Clear aff, I'm staying here,' he replied, not in the least bit interested.

'Michael, just do it. There's a heap of grass plants out there. We're going to be loaded. They're worth a fortune,' I continued.

Before I could finish my sentence, he was out the door and into the car. He reversed over to the fence, and we began uprooting the plants and shoving them into the boot of the car, aided by the dim light from the street lamp above. In seconds, we'd cleared the area of the fine shrubs and had to bounce up and down on the boot of the car to fully close it. Calmly we dusted ourselves down and ambled back into the house, where we washed the remaining dirt off in the kitchen sink. Michael and I stayed there until we got blootered as we celebrated our imminent riches.

The next morning, we headed back down to the Butler for a few pints so that we could cure our throbbing hangovers and work out how we could distribute our vast array of cannabis. We sat at the bar, innocently conversing with Don and trying not to mention that we had even been at the party in case he became suspicious of us. One patron then asked how the party had gone and if the house had got smashed up.

'It was a great night, a good crowd and very little damage,' answered Don. Then after a slight pause, he continued: 'Oh yeah, but there was a strange occurrence. Some bastard nicked all my tomato plants!'

Michael and I looked at each other and then dropped our heads on to the bar in disbelief. Our drug dealing days were not to be after all.

Since acquiring a new set of wheels, we had begun to expand our horizons even though they were old wheels that didn't spin properly.

Greg had planned to take a drive to Oxford after getting a day pass from the Mouse, so Michael suggested we load up the Anglia and tag along. Everyone had the day off as it was a bank holiday Monday. Seven of us set off from Cherry's Wine Bar. Greg and Gerry were in the front of his Ford Escort with big Tom, and I was in the back. There was no chance that I would travel in the Anglia with Michael. His erratic driving was bad enough, but with Rosie as his co-pilot, armed with bangers and blood capsules and Jonesy's extra weight on board, the short journey was doomed from the start. The bookies had stopped taking bets on the chances of a trouble-free day in Oxford. Against all odds, the old boneshaker kept pace even though the Anglia's wobbly wheels did twice as many miles as the Escort's wheels.

As we neared Oxford, things seemed to be going smoothly as we enjoyed the music of the Stranglers and other great punk bands. Before we'd left Reading, Greg had pointed out to us that the rear clip windows of the Escort were a bit dodgy and we were not to open them. Tom obviously hadn't listened to a word that Greg had said, and as we all joined in bouncing along to 'No More Heroes', he unclipped the back window to fling out a cigarette. Greg had glanced at his rear-view mirror but was helpless to prevent the inevitable.

He yelled, 'Stop! Don't do it. Don't open the wind . . .'

It was too late. The window was sucked out and was sent flying into the oncoming traffic behind. Luckily, it was deflected by the Anglia, which was immediately following behind us. We all watched as the window of the Escort glanced off the Anglia's front wing then shattered into pieces along the roadside. A direct hit had only been avoided due to the combination of badly aligned wheels, which caused an irregular side to side movement, and Michael's inability to drive in a straight line. Once in Oxford, we found a public car park near the university and tried to block up the empty window frame with an old cardboard box. Greg was muttering profanities and was not in a good mood, so Tom, Michael, Rosie, and I did a disappearing act.

I should have taken my chances with Greg because the chaos that followed almost landed us in jail. It was clear to see that Michael was in the mood for mischief. Now he was ready to let Oxford know he had arrived. We began with a dignified sightseeing stroll around St Giles as we admired the beautiful architecture and manicured lawns. A suggestion by Michael that we should visit the Ashmolean Museum had me thinking he was in learning mode. That notion soon dissolved upon finding the building was closed, at which point Michael anxiously began to scan the area for another objective.

Once inside the Silent Chapel, Michael's eyes began to flicker erratically as he conspired to perform certain acts of badness. He climbed into the pulpit and started to give a sermon. Before long, he had attracted a small crowd of tourists, and Rosie stood geared up with a collection plate. Later, we stopped at a cordoned-off shrine where we read a plaque which detailed that the eternal candle had been burning since some fat monk had lit it in the twelfth century. Michael paused, then jumped the roped barrier to the shrine, and extinguished the perpetual glow in a matter of seconds. It was childish but harmless fun. Later, out on the main street, we manhandled an annoying individual dressed up as a giant foam rubber hamburger. The oversized polystyrene person would not let us past, so he was tipped over and rolled down the hill like a bowling ball, knocking shoppers over like skittles. Fortunately, we were able to hide in a pub until the commotion died down, and by chance, we met up with Greg and Gerry.

When we returned to the car, an unwelcome conundrum awaited us. The car park was equipped with spiked ramps that dropped into the road when a car entered and then rose again until the next car approached. We needed a ticket to exit. The said item had to be purchased at a booth and inserted into a machine which would then drop the ramps, but the problem was that no one was working as it was a bank holiday. Maybe the absence of other cars in the vicinity should have been a red flag, but now we were well and truly trapped. There was no way of pushing the sharp, spiked teeth back into the ground, so we had to find another way out. The parking area was bordered on one side by department stores, so it was impossible to leave in that direction.

A row of large detached homes hidden behind a five-foot-high fence on the opposite side prevented any possibility of egress.

Or maybe not, we thought.

It was our only chance, so we chose one of the properties and prepared to attempt the great escape. Greg had a decent toolbox in his car boot, so armed with screwdrivers, a hacksaw, and a hammer, we proceeded to remove a section of the fence which led to the back garden. Rosie ran to the front of the house, opened a metal gate that led to the street, and waved us through. Then like a scene from *The Italian Job*, we screeched across the property, tearing chunks out of the lawn and destroying the vegetable garden and a magnificent floral arrangement on the way. We waved as we passed the happy family, which was having a spot of tea in the lounge, unaware that the recently caged prisoners had broken free. Before boarding the Anglia, Rosie still had time to let a banger off, which caused the incensed houseowners to duck for cover as they rushed out of their front door.

The night sky was dark and gloomy when we pulled into the underground parking below Cherry's Wine Bar. We were shivering and frozen by a chilling breeze that cut through us thanks to the missing rear window on the Escort. The turbulent ride had taken longer than usual due to the additional wind resistance, and it allowed Michael to arrive slightly ahead of us. Before parking, we double-checked that it was possible to leave through the correct channels rather than winching the cars out through the hairdresser's shop above. We relaxed over a pint and told the other patrons of our infantile pranks of the day and had a jolly good laugh.

Not long into the evening, a man entered, somewhat flustered, and addressed all the customers in the bar.

'Does anyone own a Ford Anglia parked underneath?'

'I do. Why?' replied Michael, jumping to his feet, ready for trouble.

'Well, it's on fire!' the man said.

That was the cue for a mass exodus from the bar as some patrons scattered about, worried about the building going up in flames. Those at our table scrambled to get to the car before it exploded, as did some nosy bastards who just wanted to take in the fiery affair. Plumes of thick toxic smoke billowed out from the underground car park like a funnel cloud, but gallantly we entered the fray. Yet another chap from Belfast, Big Joe, was quick off the mark and grabbed a fire extinguisher from a wall mounting. He might have been swift to pick it up, but he had no idea how to use it as he spun the canister round and round and tried to read the instructions.

'Come on, Joe. Use it. Pull the trigger!' Michael yelled.

'Give it to me you, big plonker!' exclaimed Jonesy. He tried to claw the extinguisher from Joe's grasp.

'Clear off, it's mine!' said Joe. While these two clowns were grappling with the only thing available to put the fire out, the car windows began to crackle.

Then someone shouted out, 'She's going to blow!'

Panic broke out amongst the ranks as people sprinted towards the exit signs. As we watched from a distance, she blew. All the windows exploded, sending a powerful fireball outwards into the parking bays. Before the emergency services had arrived, the poor old Anglia had ceased to be. We walked back to the bar with Jonesy and Joe still squabbling over the fire extinguisher, neither of them prepared to give it up. Michael was informed by Mr Jones that he was owed a new radio and twenty Marlborough that had been lost in the inferno. All he got was a big toe up his arse. Although the Anglia was no more, there was the pleasant surprise of a £200 insurance payout for a car that had cost £100, so Michael and I were each £50 up on the deal. Well, I would have been if I'd given Michael the £50 towards a car that I didn't know we were buying in the first place.

October had been a bitter month, and November had started off even colder. The flat had substandard heating, and it didn't help that there was no glass left in the majority of the rotting window frames. Michael started the trend of glass-breaking when he slipped at the top of the stairs after a night in the Cambridge Arms and managed to put his head though the window. If he'd fallen right through, he would have been a goner as the other side was a perpendicular drop on to the concrete yard below. Fortunately, he received only a few minor facial wounds. After Michael broke the ice, it became open season, and smashing windows became a regular source of entertainment for our clientele. Usually, a nonchalant kung fu kick was all that was required. I remember a howling wind wakening me up one night and a blizzard delivering a steady drift of snow through the glassless window frame and nestling on top of my head.

We had a couple of portable electric fires constantly burning to counteract the frosty conditions, but this ended up costing us a fortune as we had to keep filling the meter up with two bob bits. Electricity was expensive, and the more power we used, the faster the spinning wheel inside the meter turned. We had to slow the wheel down. With a carefully drilled hole through the glass panel on the front of the meter, we slid a thin needle into the wheel mechanism, but instead of slowing it down, we stopped it completely. A bonus—we now had free electricity. All we needed was one 10-pence piece to start the meter rolling, and that was it. Our landlord was a frail old man who couldn't seem to understand why there was only one 10-pence coin in the meter each time he came to collect the rent. He suspected that there was some form of skulduggery afoot but was not sure of what was occurring. We knew that he collected the rent at the same time every month and were careful to remove the needle before he arrived. We'd drilled such a minute hole in the meter glass that the old fellow never twigged that it was there. He was slightly dejected by the lack of cash in the meter, but he seemed to be downright demoralised by the lack of glass in the window frames. We weren't really bad tenants and never purposely set out to live with free electric and no windows.

CHAPTER 5

BELFAST HOOLIGAN

With no guarantee of a permanent residence and a job that I really hated, I decided to pack it all in and go back to Belfast. It was coming up to Christmas, and I did not want to spend the festive season shovelling snow off a threadbare carpet and trying to keep warm under a blanket in a squat with no windows. Also, it was quite possible that I could get my pan knocked in, trying to avoid the big grunters that the bailiffs regularly sent around to evict us. So that was it. Michael and I went home for Christmas, but I hadn't told him that I would not be returning to Reading in the New Year.

New Year's Day was the perfect time to finally lie low and hide from the demon drink. I'd just celebrated Hogmanay down at the Edenmore in Jordanstown, hanging around with my old mates, and it felt like I'd never been away. The Christmas period had also been great as I had eaten and drunk to excess with my family. Reading seemed to be a distant memory as I prepared myself for the exciting prospect of signing on the dole and avoiding the bombs and bullets of everyday life in Belfast. Michael had been going on in my lug to go back to Reading with him, but I had already planned to go to a Liverpool match the next weekend. Then the night before he was due to leave, I called him up to say I'd changed my mind and that I would also be at the airport for the plane to London. I think watching some poor bastard getting dragged from the pub the previous evening and then being kicked all over the car

49

park helped with my decision. Although I had neither a job nor a place to live, the probability of finding employment was better in Reading than in Belfast. So for a third time in less than two years, I gave my final goodbyes to everyone, and I was off on my merry way once again.

The Paul McCartney and Wings ballad 'Mull of Kintyre' still topped the charts in January 1978. Their pole position appeared reasonably safe though, with the major competition being Althea and Donna's appalling drivel 'Uptown Top Ranking' as well as the never-to-be-forgotten Brighouse and Rastrick Brass Band's 'Floral Dance'. In other earlier notable events of that year, Anna Ford become the first female newsreader, and Gordon McQueen was England's first-ever 500,000-pound player when he was transferred from Leeds United to Manchester United. Reading Football Club's fight to climb out of fourth division at that time included such stars as Mike Kearney, Mark White, Lawrie Sanchez, and Richie Bowman.

Michael still had his job at Coopers and Lybrand, but as he was without accommodation, it was a challenge for him to try to look presentable when he went to work at the office. Since he was the only person I knew who ironed everything, including his socks and underwear, he without a doubt needed a place to live. The first week back, we bummed around, staying where we could. We tried crashing at the old flat in Southampton Street, but the place was virtually derelict, and the electricity had finally been cut off. It was surprising that the premises had not been boarded up considering the amount of energy we had misappropriated from the national grid over the past few months. Marcus was still running his business from there, though he only worked the daylight hours. Thanks to the hospitality of either Marty and Jean or Joe and Gilly, who offered us the odd meal now and again, we managed to stave off the hunger pains for a while.

Nancy's brother Tom came to our rescue by offering shelter for a week and giving us a bit of time to search for our own place. He had a large elegant three-storey house in Jesse Terrace, a street that once housed people of the theatre and vaudeville acts from the early twentieth century. Tom had his own flooring company, and we thought he was a millionaire. We really appreciated his gesture to house two homeless bums. There were six bedrooms in the house plus a basement with a makeshift soundproofed music room. The insulation consisted of egg boxes stuck to the wall, which did little to muffle the amplified electric guitars and drum beats from the outside world. An eclectic array of individuals attended jam sessions in the basement, but I was surprised to find that only Tom and a musician friend named Johnny actually lived there.

I'd known that Rosie played in a band and Steve was a former drummer, but I was blown away by how talented they really were. Rosie was a brilliant guitarist who could have hit the big time, but he certainly wasn't the best to jam at Tom's house. Although I was no music expert, it didn't take a brain box to recognise the high quality of some of the local musicians, especially Johnny and another guitarist, Steve H. In addition to the assorted minstrels and hippies who attended these sessions, there were also two extremely funny chaps who could easily have walked off a Monty Python set. Simon Denning (later to be known as Slimy Simon) and Brian Sizer (later to be known as Brian) kept us entertained with various Python quotes and could recite *The Holy Grail* word for word. 'I fart in your general direction' and 'I told them we already got one' were a couple of Simon's favourites.

Brian informed Michael and me that there would soon be a vacancy at his flat and we could move in if interested. It meant sharing the same room again as we did in Southampton Street, but at least we would have somewhere steady for a while. The three-bedroom two-level flat was located above a rarely used office at 212 Oxford Road and was like a palace compared to our last place. Brian had the main bedroom but was seldom there as he was either working away or off skiing in Bavaria and other such exotic locations. The other room was shared by two peculiar individuals. They were spoilt little rich kids without jobs who were obviously dependent on their mammies and daddies for financial support. One of them was a smelly, beardy bastard who wore a long grey trench coat that he rarely took off and sometimes slept in. The other one was just a twat. Michael and I tried hard to like the two knob ends, but it was not to be. Getting rid of them soon became top of our agenda, so we decided to burn them out.

As Brian was away, we assumed seniority over our two heavy metal headbangers, who only ventured from their room to eat or shit. Michael and I were no prize winners in dish washing and general cleanliness, but our undesirable flatmates were lazy, filthy slobs. After we'd been living with them for two weeks, we decided it was time to use a wee bit of casual intimidation in order to send them scurrying back to their posh families. We picked the lock on the door to break into their room then dumped all the unwashed dishes on to their beds and neatly tucked the sheets in afterwards. That didn't work, so we soaked the bed sheets, emptied all the drawers, and then slung their clothes out of the window—but to no effect.

They were very resilient and didn't seem to take a hint easily, so we reverted to the original plan of burning the bastards out. Well, that was what Michael wanted to do, but we might have lost the flat if we'd gone in that direction. The only option left was full-out intimidation. We simply threatened to knock their bollocks in if they didn't leave, and that was all it took. With that, they despondently slouched off down Oxford Road, returning a few days later for their belongings before moving back in with their parents again. We had taught them a valuable lesson that perhaps enabled them to be better men in the future.

After spotting a small ad in the *Reading Evening Post*, I managed to get back into the lift industry after being accepted for employment by H & C Lifts. The location could not have been better as it was less than a two-minute walk to their premises. Their building was situated on the corner of Oxford Road and Western Elms Avenue, right across from the flat. The first week was perfect as I had to meet who ever I was working with at the office. But the close proximity of my employer would soon become a challenge. I had to be wary if I was given a chance to sneak home early as the risk of being spied by someone from the office was high. This was merely a minor inconvenience as I was pleased to get a second chance to complete my apprenticeship. We started to cook our own meals and live like real people and managed to obtain some stability. I assured my parents that things were looking up and that I had a real address which they could write to. They always worried about how I was surviving, so knowing that I had settled somewhere made them feel less concerned. Brian was able to put up with our madness and was really easy to live with, and as a result, things went smoothly over the first few months.

His room was like Aladdin's cave, filled with all sorts of trinkets collected from the British rail yard and roadwork construction sites. There were one-way street signs, keep-left signs, plastic cones, and an assortment of flashing lights. Various cars ended up in various holes around town. There were stories of a mad man prowling the streets by night, nicking stuff from assorted roadwork sites; I didn't want to believe that it was Brian, but the signs were all there. Brian's most prized possession was the Western Elms Avenue street sign he kept proudly mounted on his wall; he often boasted that he'd snagged the longest street name in Reading. I burst his bubble when I mentioned that Northumberland Avenue was in fact longer. When he was not around, I had permission to crash out on his bed, wearing his earphones and listening to *The Dark Side of the Moon*—magic. He was later to take me on his midnight travels as he rummaged through the parked train carriages behind the station, collecting toilet paper and some fine lotions and soaps.

A series of events meant that the good times at 212 would soon begin to fade away. One evening, I completely lost the plot whilst drinking in Cherry's Wine Bar with a few mates and some Derry men. I'd washed my hands after having a lash and was unable to release the disgusting damp towel jammed inside the wall-mounted roller. As I tugged on the blue rag, the complete unit tore away and crashed on to the floor just as one of the Derry men walked into the toilets. He accused me of busting the towel roll on purpose and started babbling on about Belfast hooligans.

'Who's a hooligan? Up yer arse, it was an accident!' I protested.

It didn't help my case when I began putting the boot into the helpless towel assembly. Before long, Tony, the landlord, came dashing in and caught me in the act of delivering the final death blow to the fiendish metal object. Incensed by what he had just witnessed, he pranced around and wiggled his fingers in the air before completely blowing a gasket.

'Right now, Mr Croft, that's it. We'll have none of that behaviour in my pub, thank you very much. Now please leave the premises.'

The staff struggled to force me from the bar and had to use an unorthodox half nelson to prevent me from grabbing various pints off the passing tables. They rolled me out of the pub across the walkway that led to the bus station, sending pedestrians scattering in the process. I climbed to my feet, humiliated by my unruly exit. My head was spinning as I clenched my fists and ground my teeth. A cloudy haze blanked out the distorted faces of the bar staff that mocked me from inside. With a surge of malicious adrenaline rushing through my veins, I stomped towards the wine bar's old-fashioned front.

I paused momentarily to take in a deep breath then shifted my neck from side to side and yelled, 'You're all a shower of miserable bastards!'

Then with a swift jab, I smashed my fist through one of the porthole-style windows, barely missing the noses of two lovebirds who were smooching within. Momentarily taken aback, I glanced at the claret stream that gushed out from my torn flesh in unison with my pounding heartbeat. Then like the roadrunner being pursued by Wile E. Coyote, I was gone and out of sight in milliseconds. I skidded to a halt in Friar Street and pulled up to grab a brown paper bag from a dustbin, which I used as a bandage to stem the blood flow from my hand. Then I made the ridiculous choice to go back to Cherry's to play it cool.

They'd think it was someone else that smashed the windie. If it was me, then why would I come back? I thought. Of course, I was a mug. As soon as I walked through the front door, I was manhandled and apprehended by the bar staff.

'Oy, what's goin' on? I never smashed yer windie,' I protested.

'Shut up, you fool! You've got a bag wrapped round your hand, soaked in blood. We're calling the police,' answered Tony.

It was a fair cop, all right; they'd done me fair and square. Fortunately, a couple of my drinking mates pleaded with Tony not to call the cops, explaining that I suffered from terminal stupidity. He agreed but banned me from Cherry's Wine Bar for life. In fact, I got a life ban from the Railway Tavern and the Jolly Porter without even stepping over the doorway as the landlords were both Tony's bum chums.

CHAPTER 6

TEARS AND LAUGHTER

Life after Cherry's was more problematic than I imagined it would be. Michael was supportive of my plight and most times joined me in trying out some drab locations for a beverage, but nearly everyone we knew still went to Cherry's. Sometimes when Michael was off with his work freaks, I'd mosey on down to the Boars Head and loiter at the bar on the off chance that someone might take pity on a lonesome soul. Ultimately, my lurking about and sporadically nodding over like a fidgety stalker in the direction of Steve Wilson paid off. He waved me over to join his crowd. Success at last—somebody to play with!

I squeezed in to join them at the corner table like it had always been my spot and was introduced to his mates. The first two that I met were Stefan Roszczyk, a stumpy-fingered diminutive hedonist of Polish descent, and then the bobble-headed Terry, who was the spitting image of Marc Bolan. That meeting changed my way of life in Reading for the better. Steve and I became best mates as I began to hang around with people from Reading rather than the Northern Irish crowd. Eugene no longer came down from London at the weekends as he had cleared off back home, and as I was barred from most of the pubs in the area, I began to enjoy the festivities in the Boars Head.

Steve came up to the flat regularly, and both of us kept fit by playing a game that we invented—foot squash—in the car park of Marley Flooring Centre, which was directly across the street. A red line centred along the building's wall and a yellow-painted no-parking zone grid made for the perfect foot squash court. Our new game was played by kicking a football against the wall, and the scoring system was similar to squash rules, only without the bats. One night, back in the Boars Head, we had cracked on with a couple of bits of stuff who were captivated by Steve's rugged Postman Pat good looks and by my high hair and the strange language I spoke. They were nice girls and declined our offer of a quick knee trembler but were thrilled that we'd invited them to watch us playing foot squash at Marley Stadium free of charge.

We had introduced ourselves to the girls as professional foot squash players and had told them that both of us had been world champions. The fact that we'd only ever played one other person—Belfast John (and he was crap)—didn't enter the equation. So the next night, the two girls turned up at the allotted time, ready with sandwiches, a flask of soup, and a blanket to keep out the swirling winds that could pick up at any time at Marley Stadium. Within five minutes of scanning the car park of the flooring company and seeing Steve and me standing and waiting with a plastic football, they were gone. It was their loss though as they were not to witness me regaining my world crown as I defeated Steve in five gruelling sets. We did invite Steve's brother John over to play our unique game, but he beat us both and became the undisputed foot squash champion of the world. Steve managed to regain the title, and we never asked John back again.

The more time I spent with Steve meant that I saw less of Michael apart from some evenings back at the flat. He was either up in London, visiting Hovis, who was recently over from Belfast, or hanging around in Caversham with some wide geezers who dabbled in various illicit substances—Dexy's Midnight Runners in particular. Michael was becoming more unpredictable than before, and his personality was gradually changing.

He no longer confided in me when he was down as he had on numerous occasions in the past. There was a deep sadness within him that he covered well, but sometimes he would tearfully break down to me. It was nearly always the same story about his father's death and the clandestine circumstances that surrounded it. He would usually open up after a few drinks, explaining that his dad had been in trouble with a paramilitary organisation.

From what I could gather from his drunken ramblings, his father had to supply a couple of hitmen with rifles. The fully loaded weapons were to be left at a predetermined location for the shooters to pick up and do the dastardly deed. Someone would almost certainly have died from these actions. Michael thought that a moment of guilt made his father have a change of heart, and he never carried out his part of the deal. The rifles were then buried at a location known only by Michael's dad, which thus prevented the hit. Michael believed that his father had a fear of a paramilitary retribution that possibly drove him to take his own life. Their last interaction was an argument; then the next day it seemed that Michael had opened the garage at his house to find his father's lifeless body. He would never get over that harrowing scene and tended to feel somewhat responsible for his father's death.

Michael could be a very soft and frank person at times, but he had a continuous struggle against the demons inside his head. Now and again he would hint that he was being challenged about his sexuality and how it was negatively affecting his life. He was reaching out for help, but I was young and stupid then. I had no time to listen to his plight. He'd had girlfriends before, so why would he be worried? I was not the therapist that Michael was in need of during those dark days of his life. When I look back, I regret being so ignorant and selfish at a time when I was his closest friend. Soon the soft side of his character began to disappear, and an arrogant couldn't-care-less attitude emerged. But he could still make me laugh.

I'll never forget the story that Michael told me about his wild adventures in London one Saturday afternoon. He was with his good friend Hovis. Apparently, they left Finch's Pub on the Portabello Road and took a stroll along Ladbroke Grove, an area where, according to Leo Sayer, you had to 'have eyes in your feet.' They stopped to admire a vintage Rolls Royce which was parked outside a magnificent old Anglican church. A wedding ceremony full of pomp and pageantry had just come to fruition, and the aristocratic guests circulated in their finery on the pristine lawns. The bride and groom were whisked away in the Roller, waving to friends and family, who were waiting in line for one of the limousines to join them en route to the extravagant reception. Beautiful women stood garnished with diamond necklaces and other priceless glistening trinkets which complemented their high-end Versace dresses. Their Armani-clad chisel-chinned partners hovered by their ladies' sides, chests pushed forwards as they posed like the big knobs they were.

Michael sauntered over to merge with the cheery throng. He was dressed in a blue T-shirt, washed-out jeans and a pair of tan hush puppies. Hovis tagged along, rubbing his bristly chin. He was clothed in his hippie finest: a green satin jacket with leather elbow patches and lilac bell bottoms with a hole in one knee. His stride was hampered by the soles of his beat-up old cowboy boots, which flapped in the wind. Brushing back his greasy shoulder-length hair, Hovis stooped to caress and then kiss the hand of an elderly lady who was wearing a coronet.

'Didn't the bride look beautiful?' he remarked to the now-blushing dowager.

'Oh, indeed, she did! Just beautiful,' she replied.

'It's been a pleasure watching her grow from a little child into such a charming lady,' he continued.

'Oh my, yes, she certainly is a special one,' said the old woman.

Their conversation was interrupted by a uniformed concierge who announced: 'My lady, your car has arrived.'

He opened the door and helped her on to the back seat. She was joined by two equally stylish elderly women, and just before the usher closed the door, she gestured to Hovis to join them.

'I think she fancies you,' said Michael with a startled laugh.

Hovis grabbed a handful of Michael's shirt, pulled him close, and whispered into his lughole, 'Shut it, Mickey. I think we're in here. Let's go for a spin.'

The pair of them slid into the back of the limo, where they were welcomed by their affluent companions. So off they went—a couple of charlatans indulging in small talk and part of a cortège of high-class vehicles headed off to a destination unknown. Next stop for the impostors was Kensington. They had enjoyed their little tête-à-tête with the gaggle of upper-crust madams, but it was now time to exit the limo and instead face the music. The ladies were escorted from the car by a captain from the Coldstream Guards, who was in full dress uniform; they were then lined up on a trailing red carpet outside an elite gentleman's club. Numerous paparazzi photographers were on hand to cover the plush wedding, and dozens of flashbulbs cracked as the guests mingled. Various members of the nobility then awaited their turn to climb the decorated stairway and make their way into the grand hall for the wedding reception.

'Who are all these people? Are they famous?' asked Michael.

'I've no idea. Maybe part of the royal family, but they've got a few shillings, all right. Stuck-up bastards,' Hovis replied.

They edged closer to the main event and stayed close to the old ladies whom they'd shared the car with, all the while avoiding eye contact with the many high-ranking bigwigs from Her Majesty's forces. Two by two the honourable guests approached the imposing foyer entrance, where they were greeted by a robust sergeant major with a full handlebar moustache. He lowered his head and listened carefully to each of the celebrated dignitaries, then stood to attention, and barked out their titles as they passed.

'Lord and Lady Snederton-Althrope.'

'The Baron and Baroness Wilmslow-Smythe.'

'The Duke and Duchess of Kathmandu.'

Then after the little old ladies went through, the pair of likely lads advanced and whispered into the sergeant major's ear. He rose and called out:

'Hovis and Mickey.' There was a slight pause. 'What? Hovis and Mickey! Who the hell are Hovis and Mickey?'

Within seconds, a platoon of Coldstream Guards had descended upon the pair and quickly frogmarched them to an emergency exit and then flung them out on to the street at the back of the hall.

They dusted themselves down, and Michael asked, 'Do ya fancy a pint?'

'Aye, OK,' said Hovis, and they were gone.

CHAPTER 7

MICHAEL BASHES THE MIDGET

After I had returned from a trip to Belfast, my relationship with Michael began to deteriorate rapidly. It started with some verbal masonry the moment I reached the flat following a brief encounter with someone as I'd walked from the bus stop.

A joker known as Kenny had nodded as he passed me and then moved along at a good pace with his head down, not looking back. It seemed a bit of a coincidence that the shifty bastard was wearing a suit jacket identical to one that I owned. When I got home, I discovered that Michael was about to do a runner as I went up to our room to unpack my case. His bed was neat and tidy as usual, but my side was a mess with old boots and smelly clothes scattered everywhere. I nearly threw up from the foul-smelling odours. I confronted Michael just as he was about to slip out of the front door.

'Oy, the room stinks. Who owns all this clobber?' I asked.

'Oh aye, Kenny has moved in,' he replied nonchalantly before disappearing down the stairs on his way to the street.

'Come back! What's goin' on?' I shouted at him.

'Up yer arse,' he replied, and he was gone.

'Yer a dick head,' I moaned, but it was all in vain.

Crazy Michael had moved his new chum into our room while I was gone for a week. Brian was a wise man as he always locked his door during his interesting adventures around the globe, but I couldn't as I shared mine with Michael. I rounded up my freeloading trespasser's rags and bunged them into a black bag and then dumped them on the doorstep. Michael got all pissed off and stopped talking to me after I advised Kenny to look for alternative accommodation; three was definitely a crowd. I let him keep my suit jacket as it now resembled something that a well-dressed tramp would have worn, and besides, a skin graft would probably be required to get it off him.

Ipswich had recently caused an upset in the FA Cup final by defeating Arsenal, with Roger Osborne netting the only goal and enabling the tractor boys to lift the trophy for the first time. Mario Kempes was setting the world alight with his marauding runs into the box and delivered a killer blow with his lethal left foot as Argentina marched towards their first-ever World Cup.

Steve and I watched most of the games together without any interruption from Michael, but we knew that it could not possibly last. During a vital game between Brazil and Peru the menace suddenly appeared with an air rifle over his shoulder.

'Where did you get that from and what are you gonna do with it?' I asked uncomfortably.

'Down the second hand shop. I'm going to shoot Marcus,' he said without batting an eyelid as he peered through the curtains out to the street below.

'Oh aye,' I said and carried on watching the match.

'There's a weird bastard sitting in a car over there. He's in the dark and looks suspicious,' said Michael, fidgeting with the rifle.

'Aye, leave him alone. He's doin' no harm,' I answered, trying to calm him down.

Moments later, the rifle was discharged; Michael had opened fire on the car. Steve and I immediately jumped to our feet to see what was going on. The driver climbed out to check for damage and looked around to see where the shots had come from. He soon found out. Michael opened fire again, this time hitting him several times about the body, but the wounded mystery man had spotted the rifle before it was pulled in from the window.

'I got him!' said Michael, grinning like a demented assassin.

'He's clocked us,' I said as we watched the silhouetted figure pulling something from the boot of his car.

He then ran across the road, brandishing a long metal tyre iron, which he then crashed through the stained-glass vision panel of our front door. The three of us sprinted down the stairs and opened the door, where we confronted a crazed bar-wielding aggressor.

'Oy, what's your game, mate? You've just bust our windie,' I said, keeping my distance in case he clunked me one.

'You just shot me!' he cried, still holding the bar aloft.

'OK, just steady on, mate. Put the bar down,' said Steve.

Just as the unknown assailant calmed down and lowered the bar, Hovis came flying down the stairs, dressed only in his jeans, and started to swing punches at him.

'*Who are we baitin'? Who are we baitin'!*' he yelled as he grabbed the startled person by the throat and pinned him against the wall.

I didn't know that Hovis had even been in the flat, but he'd been snoozing upstairs in Michael's bed since their afternoon session down at Cherry's Wine Bar. We pulled Hovis back before he could squeeze the life out of the hapless attacker. Everyone managed to get their act together as we tried to work out what to do about the unfortunate state of affairs. The unknown madman started to babble on about a drug deal he was trying to set up and how he'd be out a lot of money and maybe dead if it didn't go through. He showed us his driving licence and promised to come back to pay for the window, so considering we'd shot him up a treat, it was agreed that we'd let him go and save a lot of unwanted hassle. He cleared off, and we never saw him again.

Drug dealing was next in line as Michael continued to go off the rails. I was sitting, watching TV one afternoon, when he burst into the living room, totally off his rocker, along with the deadbeat Kenny, who had been warned not to return to the flat. They began dancing around the room, slobbering and singing incoherently; then Michael opened a long cylinder-shaped container and emptied its contents on to the dining table. There must have been at least 200 pills known as blues, the king of speed and worth a lot of money on the street. Michael and Kenny grabbed a handful each and shoved them into their gobs, increasing their animation levels as they sped out of control. I tried to settle Michael down, but he was away with the fairies. I grabbed my coat and got out.

Later I met Brian, who had not long returned from Germany. I warned him that there was a madman on the loose and that he shouldn't go back to the flat, but he was burnt out and wanted to go back for a sleep. So he decided to take his chances and head on home. I knew that I had to go back at some stage, but I tried to stay away as long as possible, hoping that Michael had wised up or cleared out somewhere. When I got back, the door was locked, and the keyhole was blocked up. I walked to the front of the flat and called up to see if anyone was home. Michael opened the window and started throwing plates at me, with most of them smashing around the oncoming traffic on Oxford Road.

'Open the door and let me in, you lunatic!' I shouted.

'Clear off!' was his response as he replaced the flying plates with cups and saucers.

I'll show the crazy bastard. I'll climb up and wring his neck, I thought.

I began to scramble up the drainpipe towards the open window. Michael countered by slinging a pot of ice cold water over me.

'I'll knock yer ballicks in when I get hold of ye!' I screamed, hanging on to the pipe like a drowned chimp.

My strength was waning, so I pushed myself up to reach the window ledge. Just when I thought I'd made it, he bashed me square on the breadbox with a large pot as I climbed through the window. Stars and wee birdies floated in circles about my head. Michael stood there, grinning, with the pot still in his hand, goading me on until I finally lost it. I leapt up and pinned him to the floor then began to punch his lights out. Brian was awakened by the commotion and ran from his room to pull us apart before I could do Michael any permanent damage, if that was at all possible. When all the disorder had died down, Brian announced that he was giving up the lease of the flat and was off to pastures greener. He said that it had nothing to do with the fact that Michael and I had terrorised the neighbourhood or that we had recently begun to tear each other's throats out. Michael assumed the lease as well as Brian's room, leaving us to have separate bedrooms for the first time since we'd been in Reading.

Things were less turbulent between us after that, and we started to hang out together again. Michael bought a convertible MG Midget, and we began to live life in the fast lane, with trips to London and out and about in the countryside. But all things must pass, and it was only a matter of time before something drastic happened. Dopey bollocks Kenny was still sniffing around Michael, encouraging him to help sell blues for a well-known drug dealer, but the problem was that he was taking more of the speed than he was selling.

My love affair with 212 Oxford Road ended when two gorillas barged their way into the flat and grabbed me by the throat. They were on the warpath and after Kenny's blood. Somehow, I managed to convince them that I'd had nothing to do with him and nor had Michael. After being manhandled, I was dropped off in a corner of the room.

Then one of them grunted, 'Tell Kenny he's a dead man walking.'

The unwelcome calling card made me think that maybe I should move on and leave Michael to it before we got croaked. We'd left Belfast to get away from all the crazies and enjoy the good life, but it hadn't taken us long to find trouble in Reading. Steve lived next door to Tom and had mentioned that his brother would soon have a room available and that I should give him a call. My mind was made up when I heard that Kenny had been found unconscious in an underground car park close to the train station with his bollocks knocked in. He was rushed to hospital and stayed there for a couple of weeks with suspected brain damage but was able make a full recovery. In fact, he was smarter when he came out than he was when he went in. Michael panicked and got out of town for a while until it all died down, and I moved to my new address: 14 Jesse Terrace.

I'd already met Stefan and Slimy Simon, the two other lodgers of the large three-story house, the place where I'd previously enjoyed music jams in the basement. It was centrally located and only a ten-minute walk from the town centre. The first days went well as I socialised with my new housemates down at the Boars Head or kicked a ball around with Steve. The move to my new digs had coincided with a switch of employment to the installation department of Otis Elevator.

As the company was located in Reading, the secretary was forever holding the phone away from her ear when she answered a call. She would say, 'Hello, Otis Reading here.'

The response was typically in song format: 'Sitting on the dock of the bay . . .'

On the Wednesday of my second week, I had gone to bed around 10 p.m. to prepare for an early start at work in Guildford the next morning. Sometime after midnight, I was wakened by the sound of the large brass knocker being repeatedly thumped against the front door. Bleary-eyed and wearing only a pair of jeans, I opened the door to see who the maniac on the other side was; it was Michael. His feet were planted firmly on the ground, but the rest of his body was swaying in a circle. Before I could say anything, *splat!* He nosedived into the hallway. The distant sound of police sirens interrupted the evening's silence, and as they neared, it became obvious that Michael was their main target. I stepped over his comatose body on to the front porch and saw his lovely blue MG Midget up on the kerb, crumpled and smoking and facing in the opposite direction of the one-way street. Seconds later, three squad cars screeched into Jesse Terrace, and the cops jumped out in haste and ran towards me.

This is not good, I thought. Two of the boys in blue were instantly all over me like a dirty shirt. One of them forced my arm up behind my back and frogmarched me out into the street.

'Oh, hold on, what's your game?' I asked.

'You're under arrest,' said one of the officers.

'What for?' I asked.

'All sorts of things,' he said.

'All sorts of things? Don't talk shite. What does that even mean? I was in bed, sleeping.'

As he tried to force me into the police car, he hesitated and said, 'You're from Belfast, aren't you? Are you a Protestant or a Catholic?'

'Am I a Protestant or a Catholic? What has that got to do with it?' I responded before breaking free from his grip.

He realised that I was pissed right off and called for me to stop, but I ignored him and kept on walking. I stood over Michael, who was still out cold in the hallway, and angrily confronted my antagonist cop. 'Why don't you talk to him? He'll probably know what you're on about.'

Almost immediately, two other cops began to drag Michael to his feet and helped him over to an awaiting squad car. He managed to come around slightly and began to wave his arms about and shout.

'Police brutality! Police brutality!'

They hadn't laid a hand on him; it was me that was getting all the bother. Most of the people in the street, including Tom, were now at their doors, watching a 'Looney Tunes Show', with Michael in the starring role. I'd been discarded by my friendly local bobby since I had faced up to him about his religious remark. The police car's doors banged shut, and they whizzed off as fast as they'd arrived, leaving the residents of Jesse Terrace mingling and mumbling to each other. A tow truck came to haul the wounded Midget away, thus dropping the curtain on the midnight pantomime.

Michael had always given me the impression that he had loads of money. As far as I was concerned, having a cheque book and working as an accountant meant that he was a smart bastard with an endless supply of cash. He was in fact knee-deep in shite. The fiasco that night when he was dragged away, kicking and screaming, by the constabulary had put him in financial ruin. Before he'd banged on the big brass knocker, he'd left a trail of destruction in his wake as he attempted to outrun the police. They had chased him through the town centre after he was spotted abusing pedestrians and weaving in and out of traffic in Friar Street. At more than three times over the legal alcohol consumption limit, he had sped up Oxford Road and smashed into a lady driving a Mercedes as she turned into Howard Street. Without stopping or slowing down, he swerved into Waylen Street and crashed into two separate parked cars before hitting one final vehicle as he crossed Baker Street. He had spun out of control in Jesse Terrace in a desperate attempt to find me and seek sanctuary. In court, he successfully made a fool out of the prosecuting lawyer, who wanted him jailed for all the offences, including driving in England with an illegal licence. The lawyer stated that a Northern Ireland licence was not valid, so any insurance policy held by Michael would also be invalid. Of course, he was wrong, and Michael eloquently let the superior court official know.

He did not go to jail but was heavily fined and had his licence suspended for two years. The judge wanted him off the road and was smugly satisfied when he handed his legal Northern Ireland licence over to the establishment. Michael was an idiot, but he was no mug as he also held an English licence that was more valuable than the one he'd given up and he knew he could use it to get insured for the road. Fortunately, he had no car any more, which was just as well. His fine, along with credit card debt, meant that he owed close to 3000 pounds, so he was positively in Shite Street and could well have ended up in jail after all.

That was the beginning of the end for Michael in Reading. Unable to earn anywhere near enough money to meet his repayments in the UK, he looked for work abroad. The oil giant Aramco fell for his inane drivel and offered him a high-paying job as he convinced them that he'd be an asset in their Saudi Arabian ventures. With a feeling of dejection, I took him to Heathrow as I was sure that I would never see my close friend again. Michael had a death wish and didn't care about the consequences of his actions, and where he was going, they wouldn't hesitate to publicly cut one's balls off for farting in the street. *Mad*, *eccentric*, and *unpredictable* were just a few words to describe Michael. He would not change his modus operandi. and after defying a couple of potentially fatal encounters, he was able to make Arabia work to his advantage.

Barely a month into his contract, he had built and concealed his own vodka still, which offered a lucrative black market niche for the many Westerners who were working there at the time. Anyone caught merely possessing alcohol in Saudi Arabia could be subjected to a punishment of several lashes. Who knows what might have happened if they had found Michael's still? He was the main man out there and had many senior administrators visiting his den of iniquity, along with Richard Downs and Marcus, who had both gained employment close to the Aramco plant. They returned with mind-boggling tales of drunkenness and debauchery as Michael burnt his crazy trail through the desert. He lived life on the edge in a country that liked to lop heads off for fun. Fortunately, he managed to keep his head, and I did get to see him again.

CHAPTER 8

OUT OF THE FRYING PAN AND INTO JESSE

The year 1979 included some major milestones. A couple of nice chaps, Idi Amin and Saddam Hussein, made names for themselves at different ends of the spectrum. Idi was kicked out of Uganda, while the upwardly mobile Saddam took charge in Iraq. Sid Vicious was found dead in New York not long after being accused of slicing up Nancy Spungen, and Margaret Thatcher became the first female prime minister of the UK. On a lighter note, people were entertaining themselves by listening to the newly introduced Sony Walkman or by playing a new game that was taking the world by storm: Trivial Pursuit. At the cinema, *The Deer Hunter* and *Superman* were must-sees. Nothing much changed in English football as Liverpool won the league for the twelfth time and Arsenal beat Manchester United 3–2, winning the FA Cup, which I witnessed from the comfort of Willie and Ena's living room. Steve cleared off with ten minutes to go and missed the best-ever finish to a cup final. Trevor Francis nodded in the winner as Nottingham Forest won the European Cup with a 1–0 victory over Malmo. But most importantly, Brighton established a nudist beach.

Life at Jesse Terrace was working out really well as I got to know new friends through Tom and Steve, although one weekend made me wonder if I'd made the right choice. We'd been in the Boars Head on the Saturday afternoon, and Stef was to take Slimy Simon, Tom, and me back to Jesse in his Ford Escort van, which he'd left in the nearby multistorey car park. Simon and I squeezed into the back of the flooring van, careful to avoid the tins of latex, bitumen, and other hazardous substances. Tom was already sitting in the passenger seat, waiting on Stef, who eventually returned, carrying a large plastic shopping bag. He seemed excited when he opened the bag as he sat beside Tom.

'Look, Tom, new cowboy boots,' said Stef proudly as the distinct smell of fresh leather filled the air.

Tom snatched one of them from Stef's grasp. There was an uneasy pause as they both looked intently at the boot; then Tom's pupils dilated like a rabid Rottweiler before he blew his top.

'You fucking bastard! First, you buy the same white grandfather shirt as me then the same light blue jeans, and now . . . *cowboy boots!*'

He kicked open the van door and stomped over to the railing of the car park then flung the boot across the roofs of the buildings below. Stef's jaw dropped as he looked behind to us for some understanding of what had just happened. Simon and I slipped back down low behind the seats with our hands over our mouths to prevent ourselves from giggling in case we got caught by the headmaster. Tom stormed back into the van and sat rigidly in silence, looking fiercely straight ahead. Stef shuffled from the van and scanned futilely for the boot, which he eventually spotted hanging forlornly from an aerial. No one spoke during the short trip back. An interesting day indeed. Tom and Stef did return later to retrieve the lonely boot.

The most satisfying part about moving to Jesse Terrace was that I got back into football again. Thanks to Steve, I was able to open up my lungs and relish a kickabout at Coley Park with his cousins, the twins Robert and Drew, and with their uncle Jim. The twins had loads of friends, who mostly came from only two families—the Harpers and the Wises—so there was always enough for a couple of sides. In fact, the Harpers had nearly enough for a team of their own, and if their sisters were included, there would be a few subs as well. They also had great nicknames, such as Cap, Daisy, Baz, H., Binner, Sniffer, and the best of all, Terry. It was great fun, but I would usually end up with bruised ankles from their uncle Jim hacking me down. I was not singled out though as he equally handed out doses of his scything tackles to anyone in front of or behind him.

Years before, Nancy and Maggie had stopped playing as he did not mind one bit booting eleven-year-old girls up in the air. Not long after the practices in the park, I went for a trial with the Reading Exiles and got selected to play. The training was hard, and the standard of play was a lot higher than I expected. The Exiles was a well-established club with a long history, and they played in the Reading and District Premier League. So if I wasn't fit, then I didn't get picked. I was at my best during those Exiles days as I reached a level of physical fitness that I'd never come close to before, and if it wasn't for Friday nights down the pub, I'm sure I'd have been even better. Alas, I looked forward to a few drinks as much as the football, so the chances of Chelsea calling on me were slim.

The summer holidays were upon us, and my parents had offered to pay for my flight to Portland, Oregon. They were visiting family, and as it was a free holiday to somewhere I'd never been to before, how could I refuse? Before I had committed to the trip, Steve asked if I fancied splitting the cost of a camper van four ways and touring the Cornwall area for a couple of weeks. It was a tough choice between Torquay and Oregon, but I opted for squeezing into a smelly fart-laden van with three sweaty males and camping in soggy fields covered in cow shit. Stef had made all the financial arrangements and picked up the converted Ford Transit van. Steve's cousin Robert was to be the other member of the crew. The van was audaciously advertised as a holiday home on wheels that would comfortably sleep four. In reality, a good night's kip in the lavish interior could only be had with someone's big toe stuffed up your nose or your arsehole.

Our cosy camper van turned out to be a delight though as we roamed the Cornish countryside without a care in the world, just glad to have some time off work. Upon arrival in Torquay, each of us bought a grotesque rubber mask and a T-shirt with the name 'The Masks' printed on it. The plan was to dupe the local lady folk of each town into thinking that we were a rock band on tour. We had some success with groupies who threw themselves at our feet, but I think they might have been falling over, laughing at us. Young Robert was the only one to have an interaction with a member of the opposite sex as he met a girl known as Liverpool Lou. She came in handy washing the dishes. Steve, Stef, and I did OK with the ladies until we took our masks off. Apart from the fact that none of us had even a sniff of a shag, the holiday was a blast. But the two weeks went by like lightning, and before we knew it, we were home.

Steve was frequently on the lookout to make a few extra bob, which he often did by dabbling in alternative forms of employment. One such adventure involved a poor old lady who was literally in the wrong place at the very wrong time. He and his pal Bob the Slob got into the furniture removal business and answered a call from a polite old woman who needed to have her house cleared. They arrived at the large house and were greeted by the welcoming old granny. Some of her belongings might well have been antiques, so they were careful not to damage anything as the items were taken from the house and on to the back of the van.

It was a long, drawn-out procedure as they carried lamps, small tables, and other knickknacks one by one up the ramp, with Bob in front and Steve slowly following in his tracks. On one trip, Bob the Slob placed an old chair on to the van and then paused. Without looking behind him and assuming that Steve would be in close vicinity, Bob raised his arse in the air and then *phraap!* He unleashed a powerful, high-velocity watery fart that rattled down his leg and out the bottom of his trousers, wafting a putrid scent of stale shite into the air.

'Pick the bones out of that one, ya bastard!' he exclaimed, shaking his leg back and forth as he attempted to release the final remnants in Steve's face. But as he swung around, his dastardly grin suddenly turned into one of alarm. There, right in the line of fire, stood the old lady holding a tray, with her grey hair somewhat singed as she had taken the full force of the massive hot fart.

'I thought you might like a spot of tea and cake,' she whispered, noticeably shaken and in shock. Steve was in the background, doubled up and rolling in hysterical laughter on the pavement.

One of the pleasing advantages of Steve living next door was that his mum, Ena, also lived there. She was a lovely lady with a rasping Glasgow accent who had made me feel welcome and at ease the very first time I walked into her kitchen. Ena had invited me to stay for dinner a few times and help Steve finish off the enormous pot of stew that always seemed to be simmering on the cooker. It was magic. That kitchen was a hive of activity, where she was frequently visited by her family, including her brother Jim, who seemed to be ever-present. Tom had a nine-year-old daughter, Suzie, from a previous marriage; she was always in her granny's house. I would benefit from these visits as I was always rewarded with a lovely hug as soon as she saw me. If I happened to be coming home from work, she would run down to greet me by jumping into my arms. Steve and Nancy had it made as they were pampered by their mum, but Tom had the best of both worlds—living away from home and spoilt rotten from the house next door! Ena certainly loved her kids.

As previously mentioned, Willie Wilson, on the other hand, was a piece of work. He was the polar opposite of Ena. He had trained his four sons in the art of floor laying, though he seemed to have discarded that trade to earn his money in rather more underhanded ways. Most of his free time was spent gambling and dabbling in occasional acts of petty criminality. On certain days, he'd get dressed in his best whistle and flute to be picked up by a Rolls Royce and head off to Lambourn Stables, where he would hobnob with the horse racing elite. He'd then stick a wad of notes on the tip of the day and return flashing the cash. On the flip side, he would be penniless a month or so later and would have to beg one of his sons for a loan.

Once, when I was talking to her, Nancy recalled a trip she had taken with her mum and dad to Heelas, an upmarket department store. Out of the blue, Willie did a swan dive down the stairs and landed in a crumpled heap at the bottom, writhing in agony. He was carefully helped to his feet by some staff members and escorted into the manager's office, where he recuperated in a soft leather chair. After a bit of negotiating, he left limping with a smug look on his face and a cheque for 1,000 pounds. It was all a show, but the store fell for it and offered him money to prevent their name from being dragged through the courts in a lawsuit. The day before, he had gone to the store and lifted a carpet edge; then on the return visit with the wife and small child, he took the deceptive dive down the staircase, all the while making sure there were lots of witnesses. One of the ways Willie made a living. Although he had been dragged up in the back streets of Glasgow, he portrayed himself as an educated man and was keen to express his knowledge, which he obtained mainly from the *Reader's Digest*.

As Nancy was the youngest sibling and only girl, it was no surprise that she was Willie's favourite child, and once that had got Steve thinking. When they were young whippersnappers, knowing of his dad's delusions of grandeur, he decided to test Willie's wisdom on the planet earth whilst the family was sitting at the dinner table.

'Dad, where does the sun shine from?' he asked.

'Ack, well now, it's quite complicated, but let me try tae explain it to ye. Light travels through the atmosphere . . .' Willie answered with a five-minute ramble. As he went on and on, Steve listened intently until he finished.

'I hope that makes everything clear to you, son.'

'Oh yes, it does, but I thought it shone out of Nancy's arse,' replied Steve, cackling as he bolted from the room.

Willie and Ena's three-storey house was almost identical to Tom's except it was much cleaner. It was such a big house for four people to live in that the large second-floor room wasn't even being used. Steve and I were about to go up to the park for a kick-around when he became curious about certain noises coming from the unoccupied room. Expecting an intruder to be on the other side, we burst into the room, ready for action. To our surprise, we found ourselves face-to-face with Steve's brothers John and Stuart, who were kneeling on the floor along with a few other people. We quickly began to feel uneasy when we noted that they were all fiddling with some strange substances. The group was comprised of four couples who flapped about in an effort to keep their illicit ritual secretive.

'Steve, you scared the shit out of us! What do you want?' asked Stuart.

'Nothing. See ya!' said Steve as he wheeled round and headed back out and on to the landing with me in hot pursuit.

'What's all that about?' I asked Steve.

'Who knows what they're up to?' he answered.

'Who are they?' I then asked.

'That group, my friend, is the Magnificent Eight. No one is allowed into their inner circle,' he said with a wry smile on his face.

That assemblage consisted of John and Stuart and their girlfriends, Carol and Helen; Dave and Anne; and Simon and Debbie.

'You have to book an appointment to speak to them,' he said, laughing.

However, I was able to infiltrate the membership of the Magnificent Eight later and become friends with each of them. Dave (or Nosher to some) was a printer and an occasional Terry Venables impersonator and would do a streak at the drop of a hat. Simon was a smooth-talking plumber.

Sex, drugs, and rock and roll was a cliché, but it was certainly what Reading was all about at that time. I had to get used to the coded jargon that the Jesse Terrace crowd talked in. At different times, I'd hear the same fidgety questions being asked about the whereabouts of certain people and when they were due to turn up. It was always the same names.

'Had Hayley been yet?'

'Had Sammy been yet?'

'What about Charlie?'

I was later informed that the three people were in fact Hayley Mills (pills, blues, etc.), Sammy (speed), and Charlie (cocaine). The eager customers would pace up and down as they anxiously waited for a fix of their drug of choice before they headed off down to the pub. Others would rather stay in if they didn't get their stash as they'd be outsiders, unable to keep up or fit in with the other high-flying muppets. I didn't believe or understand how a couple of small yellow or blue pills could give you such a buzz and transform your evening out. They said I would turn into a human dynamo and stay awake all night, impressing with my endless chit-chat any woman who came near me.

'What a load of old ballicks,' I said. 'Gimme some of those dopey pills. They'll have no effect on me.'

I took four instead of the usual two and got barred from the Rising Sun, Cross Keys, London Tavern and the Tudor Tavern that night.

CHAPTER 9

IAN THE HEDGEHOG

Residing close to the town centre had so many advantages. After only a short stroll over the bridge, which spanned the IDR on Oxford Road, you could find yourself loitering in the Butts Centre. At the end of a good old session in any of the downtown bars, a walk home saved a few bob on bus and taxi fares. One evening, I made a name for myself with my new Jesse Terrace neighbours by getting into trouble with the Thames Valley Police for the second time within a year. Not the greatest start to a new move. Most weekends, after the pubs closed at 11 p.m., those still standing would head to the night club Bryans, which was later to be known as Bones. It was an old converted mortuary with alcoves that the corpses once chilled in, which were now furnished with tables and chairs. By the end of the night, a few of the walking dead would have felt right at home. With no dress code, it was not an exotic place, which meant that if anyone was looking for a nice bit of stuff to take home, then they would certainly be disappointed. Not that any of the highly intoxicated, drooling alpha males would have been a catch for the small number of females that frequented the second-rate establishment.

I'd managed to outstay my welcome on this particular evening and found myself in the middle of the dance floor with the late stragglers, none of whom I knew. To help remind those semicoherent patrons that the night was now over, the staff would flip the switch on the main spotlights and crank up the volume to blast out 'Free Bird'. It was always the final song, and if you didn't leave within those four minutes, there was a good chance you would be temporarily blinded or deafened. The room-clearing strategy worked to perfection. Upon accepting that my night was done, I headed home alone via the market area across from St Mary's Butts church, and although I was somewhat under the influence, I still felt awake and ready to play. I kept on walking until I reached the line of silent stalls, which were ready to service the many customers at the Saturday market. Pausing momentarily, I had a peek under one of the tarpaulins. Expecting bare shelves, I was surprised to see boxes of apples and bags of cabbages hidden from the view of late-night predators.

Hmm, I thought, *free fruit and veg*. So I did what any opportunist drunk would do: I wheeled a Tesco trolley over and loaded her up. As I ambled along, whistling a merry tune, which accompanied the squeaks of my trolley wheels. Then I came face-to-face with two of Her Majesty's finest. It was a standoff.

I thought, *I'll show these clowns*. I turned to my rear and shouted, 'Run, Jimmy! *Run!*'

The bobbies took immediate action and began to sprint past me down to the stalls in hot pursuit of the evasive Jimmy. I watched the scene play out, giggling to myself as the two constables scoured the market area for young James, only to call off the chase once they were both puffing and panting. They approached to ask me if I had any idea of the whereabouts of my accomplice, to which I shook my head.

Then one of them said, 'OK then, you're under arrest.'

I was handcuffed and escorted to the police station. What a mug I was. The imaginary Jimmy had managed to give the fuzz the slip, but I had been caught red-handed. Why hadn't I done a runner when they went after Jimmy? My next mistake was not getting the services of a lawyer who might have been able to reduce the charge from theft to drunk and disorderly. Foolishly, I thought I knew better. I was sure they'd laugh it out of court. They didn't laugh, and I was stuck with a big 'Theft' stamped on my record to go along with the suspected terrorist charge still there from the Royal Ulster Constabulary in

Belfast. That charge stemmed back to a foolish decision I had made a few years back. I had been involved in a botched attempt at stealing a car and had been held by the police until they were satisfied that I was not a terrorist. Although I eventually got let off the hook, I remained on a military surveillance list for ten years.

As a result of this distressing event, I still occasionally felt as if I was a terrorist in some way, even though nothing could have been further from the truth. As for my most recent criminal charge, it was certainly a big talking point in the weeks following my arrest. I was the brunt of endless jokes from my peers, who pointed out that I couldn't get any dumber if I went for dumb lessons. I think it was Jacqui who commented that I'd had no chance as I'd been nabbed by the CID (Cabbage Investigation Department).

But life goes on. One night, after a few pints in the Rose and Thistle, I began the long, short walk home after somehow ending up on Tilehurst Road. I accidentally kicked a soft round object up in the air and was surprised to hear it squeaked upon landing. Upon further investigation, I discovered that I'd put the boot into a wee bristly hedgehog that had ended up lying on its back. The helpless little creature's legs and feet were rotating rapidly but to no avail: it was going nowhere. Feeling sorry for this spiny *Erinaceinae*, I cradled it in my arms and carried the little chap along the way, all the while being careful not to be used as a pin cushion. Then lo and behold, out of nowhere, a white Ford Escort van, driven erratically, pulled over.

Stef wound the window down. He asked me, 'Where are you going? What have you got?'

'Jesse Terrace with Ian,' I answered.

'Ian?' he continued.

'Aye, my pet hedgehog,' I replied.

He nodded. Then I jumped in for a lift back to Jesse. Everyone else was asleep, so I sneaked into the kitchen for a bowl and some bread and milk. I placed the little snack behind the wardrobe and offered Ian the nightcap before pulling the wardrobe over and securing my wee pal safely behind it. The next morning, as I was proudly showing off my new pet to the others, the bedroom door flew open to reveal a very angry Tom.

'Get that thing out of here. It's full of fleas!' he yelled then left abruptly.

That was it. Ian had to go; I couldn't argue with the big ginger. Sadly, I marched Ian to the end of the back garden then eased him over the wall into a one-time orchard directly behind and watched him scurry away. Not long after, just as I was coming to terms with life without Ian, there was a scream from next door. Then I heard my name being used in vain. Nancy and her mum, Ena, were at my front door, demanding that I go into their house to sort out a problem that I had created. Nancy had been packing a case, ready to go on holiday, when she discovered a small spikey creature snuggled into her woolly socks.

'Get your hedgehog out of here!' she demanded.

'It's not mine,' I replied.

'Oh yeah, good one. Just get it out,' she said.

'Bloody typical, I get the blame for all the hedgehogs around here!' I protested. With that, I picked the wee creature up and took him away. It might have looked just like Ian, but it was *not* him.

Though I was adapting nicely to the English way of life by hanging out with mainly friendly English-type people, I was still attracted to the dark side from time to time. One night when the pub was closing, I somehow ended up at a table alone with Mad Eddie. He was a scar-faced scary-looking bastard from Glasgow who looked like he'd been dunking for chips. He was known as Mad Eddie because first and foremost, he was mental. He talked at you rather than to you with a harsh voice that sounded like he'd been drinking bleach. Even when he was being friendly, it still sounded like he was going to knock your bollocks in. It didn't make much difference to me that he was a fruit-and-nut case as most of the clowns from my former life in Belfast were a bit unstable. This was just another character for me to spend an evening of quality time with, discussing the finer things in life.

As the bar closed, he asked, 'Do ye fancy goin' fae an Indian?'

I had no appointments marked off in my diary for that night, so I agreed to join him and partake in tasting some of the finer things that India had to offer. So off we went on our short stroll to the Agra Restaurant in Duke Street as Eddie entertained himself by throwing the head at unsuspecting passers-by.

'What are ya lookin at, ya ugly bastard?' he growled at them, cackling as they ran away, fearing for their lives.

My mistake was somehow thinking that Eddie was going to pay for the meal, and I was happy to tuck into whatever the waiters brought over to the table. In between biryanis, Eddie would lift his head and shout, 'More wine, amigo!' and then bury his face back in the plate.

After about an hour of overindulging, Eddie asked me, 'How much do you have on ye?'

'Nothin',' I replied.

'Shite, neither have I. We'll have to do a runner,' he said.

'What? You've no money?' I answered in disbelief.

'No, I thought you were paying for it. I'll go into the bogs to see if we can get out the windie,' he said, rising from the table.

Soon a banging could be heard coming from the toilets, and the waiters began to mumble amongst each other. Eddie returned a couple of minutes later, shaking his head; he then casually walked by our table, ignoring me as he paced over to the front entrance. Instantly, a waiter bolted the door, and another one bolted the door that led to the toilets. Eddie grabbed one chap by the lapels of his curry-stained white coat and threw him aside as he attempted to unlock the door. Cue the meat cleavers. From the kitchen, two burly cooks appeared with large slicing knives; they pointed directly at Eddie and ordered him to take a seat. Accepting the inevitable, he joined me at the table, muttering obscenities about ethnic minorities. I hadn't moved during the skirmish, but I finished off the wine while the sideshow played itself out. The staff held us hostage for close to half an hour, all the while refusing Eddie's requests for another bottle of wine; eventually the police arrived.

Two officers entered the restaurant, and the first one moaned upon seeing us. 'Ah no, not you again, Eddie. What have you done this time?'

The other constable asked me, 'What's your name?'

I had to think fast. 'Owen O'Neill,' I replied. I told him that I was over on holiday and was to return to Belfast the following week.

'OK, Owen, you're not being charged, but make sure you come back here to pay your bill before you leave. And one more thing, steer clear of Eddie,' he said, and that was all that happened.

They took Eddie away on a possible assault charge, but that was also dropped. A drunken Belfast–Glasgow combination in a Reading Indian restaurant was a recipe for disaster. I had felt the thrill of an evening of insubordination, but I had to be careful not to allow myself to self-destruct and ruin a possibly bright future in merry old England. A night with Eddie had given me a wayward buzz and another interaction with the law that fortunately had ended positively. Not a bad outcome considering we could have been sliced up a treat for the price of a free meal.

CHAPTER 10

TUSSLES AND BRUSSELS

I'd been in Reading nearly two years and had avoided getting my pan knocked in, which was some sort of record. In fact, I had not been involved in any major altercation at all. However, my lucky streak was about to come to an end. One night we were at a boring disco at a rugby club on the outskirts of Reading. It didn't take long before trouble started when Stef got involved in a verbal fracas with a big mouth at the bar. We didn't think much of it at the time, but when we walked out to the car park, we were greeted by a group of about twenty comedians, all of them looking for trouble; not surprisingly, the dildo who had been bantering with Stef was at the front.

'Come on. You and me, mate. Let's see who the big man is now,' he said to Stef as he minced about in a boxing stance.

It was obvious that he couldn't have fought his way out of a wet paper bag. As for the big-man comment, Stef was about five foot six, and this joker wasn't much taller. I failed to see how a round of fisticuffs would suddenly make them any taller. Stef was up for the challenge and wandered out on to one of the rugby pitches, closely followed by the group of antagonists. We stayed close. Along with Stef, there were five of us in total: Steve, Terry, me, and a hippie-type person called Martin, who had somehow gatecrashed our company. I bet he wished he'd found someone else to play with at that time though. The pair of pugilists weighed each other up, being careful to keep their distance, neither prepared to make the first move. They shuffled from side to side, then backed away from each other, then slowly approached again.

The posturing had gone on for about five minutes without a blow being struck when a girl shouted from the crowd, 'Get on with it! Somebody do something!'

That sparked some action but not much. The two fighters grabbed hold of each other's clothing and began a merry dance, eventually tumbling over and rolling around on the grass and embracing like a pair of lovers. Then Stef let out an ear-piecing squeal as he tried to remove one of his stumpy fingers from his opponent's mouth. His adversary responded by biting down even harder. Stef was now reeling in agony from the full force of the yellow molars which were gnawing on the digit like a hungry pitbull. Still they rolled around, with Stef howling as he tried to release his finger from the rabid grip of his rival.

As they continued the scrap, dopey Martin walked over to pick up an empty beer bottle that lay close to their heads. He rose with the bottle in his hand and was immediately attacked by a member of the opponents, who grabbed him by his long hair and threw him to the ground. As he began to give Martin a slap, we acted accordingly to free him, and we quickly took his assailant down with a rapid riposte. The enemy side then edged towards us under the floodlights from the roof of the main building, which swept the playing fields. The first three combatants engaged and were swiftly decked one by one as Steve began swinging. Terry and I put the boot in to make sure they didn't get up again, all the while making sure we stayed at arm's length from Steve. His eyesight was bad enough during the day, so he was just punching shadows. We could have easily ended up on the wrong end of one of his fists.

On seeing the four dead ants lying on their backs, the other group of pretenders headed for the hills; none of them seemed to fancy one of Steve's knuckle sandwiches. The scrap was short and sweet, and as we dusted ourselves down, we turned to see that the pair who had begun the initial affray was still entangled and rolling around. We pulled them apart and sent little big man scampering across the playing fields with his tail between his legs like an old hound dog. The battle was a unanimous victory thanks to a combination of Steve's shots in the dark and the away team being a crowd of yellow bastards. The only casualties on our side were Martin, who had a few bruises and a ruined hairdo, and Stef with an elongated bloodied finger.

Away from the hustle and bustle of the pub and club scene, I was really enjoying playing football. I was feeling remarkably fit thanks to a midweek three-mile run and some cross-circuit training as the Exiles prepared for a trip to Brussels. We were to play a NATO select team at their newly opened sports stadium, which was complete with swimming pools, saunas, and a nightclub. The team met at our sponsor Bill Mowbray's Greyhound Pub in Silver Street, where a coach was waiting to take us to Dover. Bill was still drunk from the night before and had to stop us at various points along the way to have a piss or throw up. It was a similar story on the other side of the channel en route from Ostend to Brussels after a session on the boat. We booked into our hotel under strict instructions from the club president to take it easy the night before the big game. Some non-players had come along just to watch, so they were ready to get wired into whatever they could get down their necks. The early start and the ensuing coach trips combined with the ferry crossing was enough for most of the travellers to hit the sack early. I was sharing a room with Steve and Greg, who had come along just to see Brussels and the NATO complex. Greg was one of the non-players who had planned to stay out a bit later, but he promised not to wake us when he got back to the hotel. Like a gentleman, he was true to his word. He didn't wake us upon entering the room but instead woke everyone in the hotel up when he bashed out his own version of 'Chopsticks' on a dusty old piano that was not for public use.

We arrived early at NATO to soak up the atmosphere of the sizeable complex and to use the many facilities available. Some of the lads had a swim or massage and sauna while others had a go at tenpin bowling until the alley was shut down when Bill and his big beer belly got wedged in one of the lanes. He forgot to let go of his ball. It took a few burly staff members to remove the drunken pub landlord, who had slithered down the lane to become entangled in the pin mechanism. When all the commotion had died down and Bill was safely tucked away in a corner somewhere, we made our way to the five-star changing rooms. I'd never played in such a lavish set up before, and the stadium itself was first class. The playing surface was like a bowling green and was surrounded on three sides by comfortable seating, with the final side having an elevated restaurant and bar reserved for the privileged few. We expected a difficult game and to be given a run-around by the athletic team of military men. Although they were extremely fit, they were no match for the highly skilled Reading boys, and we spanked them 5–2. After the win, our hosts treated us to some champagne before we headed off to take the clubs of Brussels by storm.

The evening celebrations went well but were later marred by a few of us being arrested after a late-night kick-around in the city centre, where we used some decorative ornaments as a ball. All five of us—brothers Binner and Sniffer, Steve's twin cousins Robert and Drew, and yours truly—were carted off in a large van by some very amiable police officers. That was where the cordial demeanour ended. After being unloaded at the police station, we were handed over to the very menacing leather-clad gendarmes, who were more akin to the Nazi SS. We were manhandled and shoved into a cold darkened room and left there without any idea of what our punishment might be. Later when each of us needed to use the toilet, we began to bang on the door but to no avail; they just ignored our plight. We began to constantly kick on the door until we finally got their attention. Two big hairy-arsed bastards came storming into the room, grabbed Drew by the throat, and flung him against the wall. At this point, we were allowed to use the toilets under a police escort. Drew began to yell obscenities at the guards and was taken away into a separate room, where his protests soon fell silent. We heard a cry of anguish from that room; then Drew was flung back in with the rest of us with blood spurting from his neb. One of the gendarmes had stuck the nut on him and busted his nose. It was obvious that this lot didn't mess around and that we could all get a good slap if we didn't shut up. After that, there wasn't a peep out of us for the rest of our incarceration, apart from the odd groan from Drew as he nursed his deformed snotter box. At about 4.30 a.m. a few of the nice, friendly police officers shepherded us out of the station and into a van and then drove towards the city centre.

What's happening now? we thought, but we weren't overly concerned as the evil gendarmes were not involved. When the van finally pulled over, we were each handed a broom upon our exit and were made to sweep the streets before the early morning commute began. It was a degrading but suitable punishment. Just as we began our keep-Brussels-tidy project, the gendarmes did an early morning raid on the hotel, bursting into various rooms unannounced as they searched for our passports.

This trivial event did not go down well with some of the team members who were rudely awakened in the early hours, and it was about to get worse for them. Drew and I had filed a complaint of police brutality before we left the station, and because we'd asked for legal representation, all passports were being withheld. Anyone else involved in the arrest could now be approached as potential witnesses. The club president went mental when he was told that the coach was to be delayed until the mess was sorted out. A meeting was arranged with Drew and me and the police commissioner and with the club president also in attendance. An agreement was made to release our passports if the complaint was dropped. Eventually, everything was sorted out, and the coach was allowed to leave. But the trip back was very uncomfortable as Drew and I were not very popular with the rest of the team. When we exited the coach in Reading, the president let me know in no uncertain terms that he believed I was behind all the mayhem in Belgium; he then expelled me from the club.

A few days later, disillusioned and feeling somewhat affronted by the football banishment, I contemplated my next move. I knew a couple of people on the West Reading team, so one afternoon, I decided to make the lonely slog from Jesse Terrace to their home ground at Prospect Park. I had been comfortable playing for the Exiles and felt a bit intimidated about approaching another club, considering the reasons behind my abrupt exit. By now it was lashing down, which made my day all the more miserable. My gloom hit rock bottom when a flash git driving a Porsche splashed through a puddle before screeching to a halt by my side. I was already wet, but this wanker made sure I was well and truly soaked by displacing the contents of the puddle all over me.

He wound down his window and asked, 'Oy, chief, what's the quickest way to Windsor?'

'Are you on foot or in the car?' I returned.

'In the car, of course, you dick,' he snarled.

'Well, that's the quickest way,' I replied and walked on, feeling a wee bit better about myself.

CHAPTER 11

ALAN BALL LOVES SCAMPI

The Exiles may not have wanted me, but you can't keep a good man down. The next season, I signed for West Reading, a team also in the premier division, and smashed the league's previous record transfer fee between clubs. The price to move my majestic talent from one club to another doubled, rising from 3 pounds to 6 pounds. It was then that I found out to my dismay that rather than receiving this windfall, I actually had to pay it to join another club. Halfway through the year, I was again out of pocket after another move following a disappointing campaign with West Reading. Simon had convinced me to drop my standards to join his team, United, a squad from the combination league which played its games at Cintra Park.

My first game with the no-named (just United) team had me shaking my head in disbelief as I wondered why I had made such a move. We kicked off, and the ball was played back to one of the midfield players, who passed it back to the centre half. He in turn spun round to whack the ball over our goalkeeper's head for one of the fastest own goals in history. What had I done to my career? It got better though, and the team would eventually become a strong force in local football with the backing of various pubs, including the Fives Bar, Horse and Jockey, and then finally, the Roundhead. It was then that we moved from Cintra Park to play at Coley Park, where the Roundhead was located. Later I was able to drag Muff and Dickie away from the pub at the weekends to join me in the Horse and Jockey side.

Saturday afternoon games were very competitive, and I kept fit by training twice a week to make sure I made the first team. One notable game had a banner headline in the *Reading Chronicle* following a 6–0 victory. It read: 'Horse and Jockey win at a canter with goals from the Three Wise Men'. It went on to praise brothers Eric, Dave, and Rob Wise on each getting a goal. I was not mentioned in the article despite having a corker of a game and netting the other three goals to complete a perfect hat-trick. It was the story of my life.

A lot of the top players in Reading also showed off their football skills in the Sunday morning league. Foolishly Muff and I were talked into joining the TUC Club to play the final few games of the season. Although the standard was very low in the league's sixth division, I thought it might help improve my Saturday performances. What I had not allowed for was that the kick-off was at 10 a.m., meaning that we would still be drunk from the night before. It was a disaster, but I did win the leading goal scoring trophy that was presented by World Cup winner Alan Ball at the old Trade Union Club in Minster Street. He appeared under the condition that no press would be in attendance and that members would refrain from taking photographs.

When handing me the trophy, he squeaked in his croaky voice, 'You won this with seven goals. You didn't win the league then?' He chortled sarcastically.

'No, we didn't, but I only played five games!' I replied and joined him for some scampi in a basket.

That was to be my one and only season in the Sunday morning league. Alan explained to me that he hadn't had scampi in a basket, his favourite light snack, for quite a while. Apparently, during his time playing for Blackpool, he would often feast on a portion of the little shrimp delights, but when he joined Everton, he did not indulge himself. The idea of anything in a basket was put on hold when one of his Scouse teammates badly burnt his legs when trying to tuck into some extremely hot soup in a basket.

For those who have limited football knowledge, Alan Ball was a leading light in English sport during the 1960s. Soon after England's celebrated victory against West Germany at Wembley, Alan Ball had signed for then FA Cup holders Everton. A late goal from Derek Temple saw Everton fight back from a 2–0 deficit against Sheffield Wednesday to win 3–2 in the 1966 cup final. That team of the late sixties became a force to be reckoned with, with a strong midfield consisting of Colin Harvey, Howard Kendal, and the tireless Alan Ball himself. They were affectionately referred to as the Holy Trinity. This was the beginning of a period of dominance for this great side. Although they lost the 1968 FA Cup final to a screaming left foot drive from Jeff Astle against an inferior West Bromwich Albion team, Everton were to become champions of England two years later. Alan's timing in most games was second to none, but he was not so clever when moving from one club to another. He was to miss out on another FA Cup medal when he moved to Arsenal shortly after their league and cup double in 1971. Arsenal did reach the final again the next year, but Alan was to be a runner-up for a second time in a 1–0 loss to Leeds United.

Alan modestly declined my offer to join Muff and me in the TUC midfield to establish the New Holy Trinity, perhaps worried that we would overshadow him. He could have had scampi in a basket every week, so it was to be his loss. He would also miss Saturday football action and the rise of United FC when he also snubbed that offer. Alan Ball might have had his reasons for not signing for the Horse and Jockey, but I'm sure he regretted his decision not to have joined such an exciting team. They soon became a force to be reckoned with in the Reading Combination League as they outplayed most of their opposition with ease. Alan most certainly would have kicked himself when he found out that he could have been enjoying a game of cards and a few pints down the pub after the match. The Horse and Jockey was run by the former Reading forward Mike Kearney and his wife, Grace. They would allow team members only into the pub a couple of hours before it officially opened its doors. We felt honoured to be waited upon by such a lovely Scottish couple as we laughed at the curious punters outside looking in and wondering why we were getting preferential treatment.

Mike had been part of the Reading squad of 1978 that defeated the first division's Wolverhampton Wanderers in the league cup on a famous Wednesday evening at Elm Park. Steve and I had been squeezed into the compact old ground that night, and we witnessed striker Pat Earles netting the only goal to send Reading through to the next round. Mike was later to play alongside future stars, such as Kerry Dixon of Chelsea and England; Neil Webb of Manchester United and England; and Lawrie Sanchez of Wimbledon and Northern Ireland. Lawrie later went on to be an FA Cup hero when he headed the winner in a 1–0 victory over red-hot favourites Liverpool on my birthday in 1988. Of course, things might have been different if John Aldridge had put away an earlier penalty that was saved by the legendary Wimbledon keeper Dave Beasant. Some of these Reading greats, which somehow included Eugene, were given honorary club membership by Mike, who allowed them in for a sneaky drink before the pub opened. In fact, Martin Hicks was a regular early hour's tippler, but we drew the line by not allowing him to be part of the card school.

Historically, Jimmy Greaves, Frank Stapleton, and George Best were just a few of the players from the 1970s and 1980s who were rumoured to have had a penchant for scampi in a basket. Apparently, Peter Osgood and Kevin Keegan preferred sausage and chips in basket after a run-out at the Bridge or Anfield respectively. It is thought that Peter Taylor was the one behind the gammon-steak-and-pineapple-in-a-basket craze enjoyed by that Nottingham Forest side of the late 1970s. In fact, that diet might have helped the team go on to win the league championship and two European cups under the management of the late and great Brian Clough.

Modern footballers now have dieticians who instruct them on what and when to eat. Not so for the early pioneers of the game, particularly one William 'Fatty' Foulke. He was six foot four and weighed twenty-four stone, and although he did not move about much, his large frame would have taken up most of the goal area. Foulke played for Sheffield United, Chelsea, and Bradford and won an England cup in 1897. In thirteen years, William Foulke captained Chelsea, won the first division title and twice won the FA Cup—not bad for a 'fatty'. Sadly, this not-so-healthy sportsman died at the young age of forty-two in 1916. Football fans are constantly on the lookout for any player who has been overindulging, and it will not take them long to let the fat ones know about it. The chant 'Who ate all the pies?' would soon ring out around the stadium. The slightly-overweight and much-travelled Micky Quinn was constantly serenaded with a rendition of 'Who ate all the pies?' During a game when playing for Newcastle against Grimsby Town, a fan threw a pie on to the pitch, and to the delight of the crowd, Quinn swiftly picked it up and ate it.

CHAPTER 12

MONEY DOWN THE DRAIN

Property in Reading town centre was at a premium. Many places around the Kennet Canal—the old Trade Union Club amongst them—had been earmarked for demolition in order to make way for the future super-development complex the Oracle. Not surprisingly, Willie Wilson managed to pick up a lease on the top floor of an unused building in Duke Street, with the plan to open up a pool club. No one knew where the money to finance such a scheme came from, but somehow, he and another dodgy character set the wheels in motion. As Steve's dad would be the owner of the club, Steve assured me that we would be spending a lot of time there, partaking in a few beers and free pool games whenever we wanted.

The opening night of the Duke was brilliant, with beautiful girls in miniskirts promoting Foster's Lager and handing out gifts. They also set up a yard of ale contest to see who could finish one of the oddly shaped bulbous glasses in the quickest possible time. Being a somewhat slow drinker, I didn't see any reason to take part in the competition, but when I heard that the first six people could enter for no charge, my name was soon on the list. Dave and another throatless wonder gulped the golden liquid down their necks in no time at all, but the race was too close to call, so they had to have a drink-off. As if they hadn't consumed enough alcohol in record time, they lined up another pint of Foster's each, with Dave ultimately triumphing by a matter of milliseconds. They also won another contest by becoming completely blootered before anyone else. My finishing time of about ten minutes left me firmly in last place, but I only entered for the free beer.

Steve, Nancy, Stef, and I helped Willie out in the early days by working behind the bar for no wages, so initially the place was turning over a nice profit. It was hard work, but we had a good laugh doing it. My first night was also the first time I'd ever served anyone, and a middle-aged couple sat at the bar to order some drinks. She was wearing a long white dress showing plenty of cleavage, so naturally my eyeballs were fixed on her ample melons as they rose up and down with every breath. She ordered a vodka and orange, he a bottle of Guinness. The man was waffling on about some old shite as I poured the fine lady her drink, but his conversation was just muffled background noise because the main show was obviously her big tits.

He was still babbling on when I grabbed his Guinness from the shelf, ready to take the lid off, using the bottle opener attached to the countertop. I'd seen bar staff in the past busily shuffling around, opening beers with a quick flick of the wrist, and then offering them to their thirsty patrons. When I attempted this sleight of hand, it went spectacularly amiss. Instead of the old wrist flick trick, I inserted the bottle upside down to release the top, but alas, the angle of entry was a recipe for disaster. This elevated position created a pressure chamber of bubbling crude. A high-velocity stream of the black stuff cascaded out from the bottle and exploded like a water bomb on the woman's ivory bosom, staining her beautiful white dress and almost knocking her off the stool.

Her partner went berserk. 'You stupid bastard! You've ruined my wife's dress. I'm going get you fired for this!' he exclaimed.

'Aye, go ahead then. I'd love to get fired from a job that doesn't pay me,' I replied.

I thought he was going to chin me when I attempted to wipe the remainder of the creamy suds from the woman's chest. Fortunately, he turned and escorted his wife from the bar, ranting and raving and shaking his fists in the air as they left. Not a bad start to my inaugural bartending show. As with anything, time was all I needed to positively take up the wage-free challenge. In fact, as my confidence behind the pumps grew I became infected with a slight dose of megalomania, which peaked when I barred someone for abusing his girlfriend. I then used my position to assist the poor damsel in distress, offering her a shoulder to cry on and perhaps a comfort shag. All I got was a belt on the bugle.

I was much better at pool than I was with women. As promised, Steve was able to pick up the keys of the club and most days we would head there during closing hours to knock the balls about. As a result, our games improved vastly. I managed to win a couple of tournaments hosted by the Duke Club, snagging a couple of cash prizes and a big furry panda in the process. The problem was that I'd promised the panda to a few different girls if I won it, so I had to sling it before any of them found out. I was probably the best player in Reading at that time, if I do say so myself. As the year ended, Steve began dating a young girl called Anne, one of four sisters from an Irish family, so our pool days slowed down a bit. It was obvious that he really liked this girl, and I did not see as much of him as before. One night I knew it was the beginning of the end for Steve and me when I caught them lying down in front of the dartboard, measuring each other's height using the rubber mat distance markings.

A couple of seedy nightclubs were due to close their doors in order to prepare the buildings for demolition during the first phase of the Oracle's construction. The owners of one of the clubs were well known in Reading's criminal underworld and had eyed up the Duke as a replacement. Steve and I were sitting in his parents' front room one night when the phone rang. I answered it.

'Is Willie Wilson in?' asked someone with a muffled voice.

'No,' I replied.

'Is that one of his sons? Tell him there's a man in town with a shotgun and he's going to blow his knees off,' continued the muffled voice.

I paused, then turned to Steve, and said: 'It's for you.'

By the time Steve got to the phone, they'd hung up. Someone was possibly trying to put the frighteners up Willie in order to get him to hand over his club. We ignored the threat, but Steve let his dad know about the call. Still, all things must pass, and the Duke eventually changed hands when a couple of gangsters bought the lease for next to nothing after finally turning the screws on the owner with some heavy intimidation. The holder of the title was now Willie Wilson's former partner. Willie was a sneaky bastard and knew of the impending threats, so he sold off his shares for a healthy profit before the aggravation occurred. But we'd had enough free drink by then, so it mattered not.

The year ended in Belfast when I invited Steve, Stef, and Nancy to join me for Christmas to stay with my parents so that they could see the Ulster Troubles up close and personal. Before that, we stopped off in Glasgow for a night with Steve and Nancy's grandparents, who lived in a multistorey flat in Partick. Stef was excited about the trips to both Glasgow and Belfast as he got a strange high about having a drink in places he felt quite intimidated in. We left the Wilsons' lovely granny before heading off for a pint with their grandfather Tug, a squat but near-identical version of Willie in both looks and personality. Off he marched at a high pace, leaving us in his wake as he meandered through the side streets of Partick on the way to his local pub. Upon entering the seedy tavern, Tug was still motoring at high speed as he made a beeline towards some of his cronies at a corner table. The four of us halted at the bar, noting that one of us was going to have to buy the drinks as Tug certainly wasn't going to put his hand in his pocket.

Stef decided he should get the first round and nervously called, 'Tug, what do you want to drink?'

Without batting an eyelid or acknowledging that Stef was even in the bar, Tug replied, 'A half and a halfen.'

Stef stood still, baffled by the response. 'What does that mean? What does he want?' he asked uneasily.

'He wants half a lager and a whisky chaser,' I answered.

'How do you know that?' he enquired.

'I just do. They say the same thing in Belfast,' I replied.

Stef manoeuvred his way through the bar to get the drinks, and we sat at a table, surrounded by red-faced gorillas and seasoned drinkers.

Tug was an impeccable host; he totally ignored us, instead choosing to sit with his friends at a different table.

Stef surveyed all around him and, as he picked up his pint to take his first sip in a Glasgow pub, said, 'I don't know what you were all going on about. Glasgow's not that tough. There are no hard men in here.'

Just as he'd finished his sentence, a man standing directly in his eyeline got a fist full of fives from a fellow known locally as Wee Mental Mickey. The direct hit busted his nose open and sent him sprawling across our table, smashing glasses and sending blood, snotters, and lager into the air.

'And what were you saying, Stef? Welcome to Glasgow,' said Steve as he casually wiped some beer from his lap.

Fortunately, our time in Belfast was limited to a couple of minor incidents. Steve dodged a bullet (no pun intended) when he inadvertently helped himself to a fellow's cheese in a downtown bar, thinking that the plate was for all to share. Then Stef was nearly shot by my dad when he arrived home late one night after getting lost and tried to awaken Nancy by banging on the window with a large pole. With a lack of explosions or murders to witness in Belfast, we were back in Reading for the New Year, and I celebrated Hogmanay with a final swansong at the Duke.

After being together a lot over Christmas, Nancy and I began seeing each other regularly in what was destined to be a doomed relationship. Various factors caused the failure of the midwinter fling: we were too young, I was an eejit, and she was a crazy woman. If only we had spent less time slapping each other about and more time concentrating on the romantic aspects of a relationship, then it might have been a success.

In the few months that we were together, we tried to act like a loving couple, but our immaturity was to get the better of us more times than not. Ultimately, the main reason for our break-up was a communication breakdown. When we went out, we were always in the company of dozens of other people so one-on-one time was at a premium. Maybe if we had gone away more often, things might have turned out differently.

I remember a trip to Southsea we took once. It was a weekend of nothing but fun and laughter as we frolicked on the pier and in the amusement park, soaking up the atmosphere like children. Maybe getting a photograph taken with a monkey was a bad idea. It was obvious that the cuddly primate was ill at ease with the photoshoot and franticly bounded from our arms to the sanctuary of the next couple waiting in line. We almost certainly shared our best moments during that trip. Unfortunately, when we were back in Reading, we always ended up surrounded by so many people that we were rarely alone. Whether we were at my place or hers, there were always people everywhere, and gradually our communication got worse and worse.

On top of all that, Nancy was under pressure trying to deal with the continuing altercation between her mum and dad. Willie was impossible to live with at the best of times, but eventually Ena decided that she'd had enough and moved out to stay with John, who lived just around the corner in Baker Street. Willie then expected Nancy to replace Ena and wanted her to cook for him and clean the house when needed. It was not the first time that Ena had left Willie, but she usually returned after a few days, probably in fear that he would track her down and drag her back home. This time Ena seemed much braver and was determined to stay away for an extended duration. Willie was worried that his wife might never return, which in turn made him feel sick.

He had been coughing up blood from an ulcer in his stomach and was in fear that he might be terminally ill. This was highlighted one day when Nancy returned to find bloodstains on the bathroom and hall floors. Ena was told of Willie's condition but held firm at John's house. The other four siblings were fully supportive of their mum, knowing that she would be content living with John. Eventually, though, Ena did return, possibly concerned that if Willie did die, she would never be able to forgive herself.

He did not die, but he must have believed that he was going to. What he was to do next would not have been done by a rational human being. A while back, he had had a big win on the horses—close to 10,000 pounds—a matter that he kept to himself. As he was now convinced that his time upon this earth was numbered, he flushed the money down the toilet as apparently this was preferable to leaving it to Ena. He never for one moment imagined that someone else in the family might have needed a bit of financial support. Nor did he consider donating the money to charity. Eventually, upon realising that he was not going to die, Willie disclosed to Nancy what he had done. Nobody quite knew what was going on inside Willie's barnet, but he and his wife were ultimately reunited. For many years after that, Nancy believed that the blood on the bathroom and hall floors was in fact red dye that Willie had strategically smeared around, hoping for a sympathetic reaction. On the upside, I'll never forget the extraordinary story that the *Reading Evening Post* published about the sudden emergence of numerous twenty-pound and fifty-pound bank notes from drains all around the town.

CHAPTER 13

AN INVITING SLICE OF CHEESE

The New Year had us singing along to the Pretenders, who topped the charts with 'Brass in Pocket' ahead of a couple of gems: 'Another Brick in the Wall' and 'London Calling' by the Clash. And who could forget the classic 'Day Trip to Bangor' by Fiddler's Dram? The world became infatuated with the Rubik's cube, the Winter Olympics opened in Lake Placid, and the Audi Quattro was introduced to the echo of 'Vorsprung Durch Technik'. We would also be endlessly entertained when Trebor Ebagum was elected prime minister of Zimbabwe. In one football first division game, league leaders Liverpool defeated neighbours Everton 2–1 at Goodison Park. Before the game ended, Merseyside was to lose one of its legends when Dixie Dean suffered a heart attack in the stands and died at the age of seventy-two. Ipswich Town all but ended the title challenge of Manchester United by spanking them 6–0 at Portman Road.

With Steve now in love and missing in action, I had to find someone else to play with. Dave and Big Simon (not to be confused with Slimy Simon) were often round at Jesse Terrace when they weren't involved in covert Magnificent Eight activities, and they would join the rest of the crowd for a drink or two in the Boars Head. A few weeks before my banishment from Cherry's Wine Bar, I'd played pool and become good friends with a butcher called Chris. He disappeared for a while then turned up one day with a few old school friends, showing off his badly damaged hand, which he'd sliced up a treat on an exceptionally sharp cutting tool at work. But that was it for Chris; he vanished again and became a virtual recluse, but some of his friends continued to join us at the weekends.

Muff, yet another Simon known as Gus, and Dickie were the first of a crowd that gradually increased each week until it was very expensive to buy a round. Times were changing, and the increase in clientele made it imperative to get to the pub early. Instead of a handful of people occupying a corner table, there would now be close to fifteen jostling for a seat. By chance, a bearded barman called Jamie helped us out by knocking a few quid off some of the larger rounds. By evening's end, he would indulge in a strange ritual of going around the tables and finishing off any untouched vodkas and gins.

Our original crowd of old farts in their twenties got on like a house on fire with this new group of young bloods, who were in their late teens and freshly out of schools such as Stoneham or Ashmead. When the word got out that the entertainment level at the Boars Head had reached peak levels, even more of the new group began arriving. An added attraction was provided by Muff and me each time the Jags' 'I've Got Your Number' was played on the jukebox. As soon as the first few bars were belted out, the two of us would bounce from the crowd and jump about like two raving loonies, singing along until the last note. Then just as if a switch had been flicked off, we would halt and simply blend back into the crowd to continue what we had previously been involved in. It might have been an irritation to some, but we loved it. A few of the new associates were given nicknames which we thought suitable at the time. These happy-go-lucky chaps included Pete the Cheat (named by Eugene when he was caught cheating at pool in Southsea), Deano, Andy, Paul Cabbage (labelled by Simon after he was in a car accident), Shaggy, and Smelly Bacon (named after a bacon sandwich).

There was also a young motorbiking high-flyer called Neil, whom I christened Orange Peel because it was my turn to pick a nickname. He was a real livewire and, after a dodgy start, was soon accepted into the fold. It didn't hurt that he lived in a nice big house that his mum, Anne, kindly opened up to us or that his dad owned an Aston Martin and a Ferrari. One night when he asked if anyone would like to have a go in the Ferrari, I began throwing punters behind me to get to the door first. To my dismay, the trip did not entail that I would be able to drive the gleaming electric-blue supercar. Instead I had to settle on being compressed into a miniature backseat for a forty-mile round trip to and from Slough with Neil as a passenger and his dad driving. We were back within a handful of minutes, but what a ride!

It was coming up to Easter when most of the amateur football clubs began preparing for their sorties to Belgium. Because of my recklessness, the previous year I'd been banned from travelling with the Exiles, so I was prepared to miss out on the continental extravaganza. Someone suggested that we should organise a trip to Amsterdam, totally independent of any football clubs. None of us had been there before, and by the time all the bookings were completed, there were at least ten names committed to the excursion. We arrived in Amsterdam to accommodation that happened to be in the middle of the red-light district, where it was a prerequisite to get wasted on whatever was available. That part of the city was a haven for a collection of crazies, and there was hardly a Dutch person in sight.

An assortment of eccentric vaudeville acts was on display, from street buskers to mime artists, all of them two bob short of a guilder. For a minimal fee, strip bars offered as much beer as you could drink within half an hour of purchasing a ticket. Twenty minutes into the session, most punters were so blootered they did not realise that a heavy penalty would be accrued for every minute past the cut-off time. It got pricey. Whilst sitting on bar stools at one club, we were merrily chatting away to a couple of Welsh rugby players. One of them became startled and knocked his beer over as he spun around to find an exotic lady of the night giving him a blowjob without his permission. He had a dangerous person on his weapon. Later we were invited to partake in an array of fine marijuana substances from a robed man who could have easily stepped off the set of *Casablanca*. He had a drop-down tray attached to his chest similar to that of an ice cream usher at the cinema.

The place was spinning. It was pandemonium, full out drinking, shagging, and snorting. Every other girl we met was either a hooker from such outlandish locations as Sunderland or Gdansk or just simply an absolute nutter. Four days was long enough in the city where one could obtain or catch anything that was available. The flight back to London was surreal as most of us were already riding a high, and whizzing through the clouds only exaggerated it. When we landed, it was a comedown in more ways than one.

On the completion of our foray into the twilight zone, we returned to the real world, nervous and twitching. Some of us had tattoos of strange faces on strange places of our bodies, while others had lost the ability to talk. Four days of our lives had vanished out there, gone from the memory bank forever. A few of us began to fear the unknown as we'd intermittently go into odd spasms or shake uncontrollably. These unexpected contractions could happen anywhere—in restaurants or when walking innocuously down the street. It was a disturbing time that could never and should never have been repeated.

After the trip to Amsterdam, there had also been some lingering tension between Eugene and Gerry. I eventually learned that it stemmed back to the voyage that the two of them had taken back from Amsterdam together. They had chosen to slum it by taking the boat and the train as they tried to save a few bob. They had arrived in rough condition, looking like they had been trampled by a herd of Japanese water buffaloes. The journey back was to be much worse. The ferry ride across the channel was a brutal one with second-class voyagers throwing up all around as the boat heaved and fell in the murky surf. Angry nimbus clouds showered the vessel with a torrential downpour along the way, mixed with the odd lightning bolt that danced on the sea nearby. Ashen-faced and miserable, the two of them stopped off at a transport cafe when in England. They were not the greatest travelling companions at the best of times, and it would only get worse. They had budgeted not to spend much money during their trip, but Eugene's spreadsheet was off by one day; he had no money at all. Gerry being Gerry showed no sympathy towards his ravenous partner when they entered the cafe.

Eugene looked up at Gerry and, with his best *Oliver Twist* expression, begged, 'Please buy me some breakfast!'

Gerry looked into Eugene's doe eyes and grumbled, 'Your eating days are over, man.'

Not a word was spoken as the pair shared a table. Gerry tucked into bacon, eggs, sausages, beans, fried bread, toast, and tea. Eugene sipped on some lukewarm water from a dirty glass. Following the uneasy repast in the cafe, they boarded the train to London without making any further conversation. The travelling inventory included a prepaid ticket from London by train as well as the ferry crossing, but the last leg to Reading would be a separate fare. By now both were penniless. Eugene made a reverse charge call to see if he could be picked up. Gerry stood hushed and just waited. In due course, a car arrived to take Eugene to Reading, and he climbed in without acknowledging Gerry's presence. Before the car took off, Gerry finally opened his mouth to ask Eugene if he could get a lift with him.

Without turning his head Eugene replied, 'Your travelling days are over, man.' And with that, he was whisked away by his driver.

Meanwhile, back to the somewhat reality and stability of Jesse Terrace. Tom opened up a room of the top floor, which had previously been filled with old exercise equipment and junk, thus allowing the population of Jesse Terrace to increase by one. The faces were also changing as Slimy Simon and Stef moved out and Big Simon, Muff, and Gus moved in. This allowed me to take over the master bedroom, which was complete with a grand piano and French windows that swung out on to a veranda—very majestic indeed. Although this was the largest and finest room in the house, it also had its shortcomings. The French windows could easily be forced open, so when someone forgot their key, the gateway to the rest of the house inevitably was through my bedroom. That didn't bother me though as my worldly possessions could have slid comfortably into a brown paper bag and I didn't have two bob to my name so I figured my chances of being robbed were slim.

Brian was a regular French window intruder and would frequently appear on the veranda, announcing, 'I'm coming through the window. I've got a Tesco trolley!' He always seemed to be popping up, pushing trolleys around.

One night, I left the pub before closing time and was in bed and out for the count in no time at all upon returning home. In the early hours of the morning, something appeared to be irritating my sleep pattern, and I was unsure if it was a bad dream or not. Slowly I began to waken and opened my eyes to find some strange hippie-type people sprawled out across my bed. Others were dancing to music that was being played from my digital alarm clock radio player. There must have been twenty people in total. Dave had invited them back for a party in my room but hadn't considered it necessary to wake me and ask if I wanted to be involved.

It would not be long before 14 Jesse Terrace established itself as the centre of the sex, drugs, and rock and roll universe, with all sorts of shenanigans occurring. We all became very good friends and trusted each other with most things, but if anybody brought a woman back, then it was every man for himself. If you needed a piddle in the middle of the night, it was not uncommon to return to bed and find that one of the other residents had taken your place. Other times, after a good shag, it was possible to wake up with a different girl or maybe even an extra one! There were many lovely ladies who graced the halls of Jesse Terrace, some of them with very exotic names that might or might not have painted a picture of what they truly looked like. Fine women such as Chicken Legs, the Brown Dog, Slanty-eyed Anne, the Milkman's Daughter, Donkey Lips, Frog-Eyed Sprite, Biffo the Bear, and last but not least, the Gift-Wrapped Gorilla.

The going rate to rent a room at Jesse Terrace was ten pounds a week. And although it was not extortionate, times were hard, and wages were low. So there was never much food in the larder. Tom though had stacks of cash and ate well; he had a particular penchant for fine cheeses. He usually had someone pick up his weekly shopping supplies, and amongst these delicate delights would be a large block of cheese that he, of course, kept in the fridge. On one such occasion, after the shopping spree, I sneaked up to the kitchen late at night with a rumbling in my belly and a craving for some sustenance. Carefully I eased the fridge door open and spied the succulent slab of golden cheddar, which was inviting me to take a sample. My nose was twitching like a curious house mouse as I inhaled the tempting pungent bouquet.

No one will ever know if I slice a tiny wafer from this imposing block, I thought. In an instant, I carved an edge off, making sure that the block remained neat and square, and then slid the scrap down my neck. The next morning, we were all awakened from our peaceful slumber by the sound of Tom's booming voice echoing throughout the hallway:

'Who's been eating my fucking cheese?' he yelled.

I rubbed my eyes and crawled from bed, not believing that he would have noticed the little morsel that had been removed from the giant block. Although I was slightly concerned about a confrontation with the big ginger, I decided to own up and save the skins of the others and take my punishment like a man. But it turned out that everyone else had made the same late-night sortie into the kitchen, each removing a slice and thinking the same as I did—that he'd never know. After we'd all done the deed, there was barely enough left to fit on a cocktail stick with a pickled onion. The fallout for this misadventure was that we were all in big shite; Tom's fridge became strictly out of bounds, and we had to organise our individual food storage locations. Secret stashes began to appear around the kitchen area, with chosen cupboards hijacked and warning signs posted on doors: 'Keep Out or Else'. Provisions were hidden in an old washing machine, a linen basket, a broom closet, and other unhygienic places, particularly under Muff's bed. All sorts of bacteria and strange creatures were living in discarded pots and pans and dancing around spoons and forks which were wedged into hardened leftovers like maypoles. Muff was a bit of a bin hoker and was caught on various occasions dusting off slices of toast for an evening snack from the rubbish bin.

One little lady was obsessed with Muff and obviously not too concerned about the unhygienic state of his bedroom. She had bought him a beautiful black T-shirt with a classy silver crest of the Police (the band) on it. I was jealous but couldn't afford to buy one, and Muff knew this.

The next time she was visiting, he asked her, 'Do you love me?'

She swooned and said, 'Of course, I do, Muff.'

'If you really love me, then buy Crofty a T-shirt,' he requested.

I didn't get one, but I knew he meant well.

The front and back bedrooms on the main level were in fact one large room that Tom had divided by installing a false wall. He had suggested that I should attempt to decorate the drab grey plasterboard sections in order to enhance the feng shui. Painting it seemed to be the best option, but it would be at my cost, so I had to come up with a cheaper alternative. It was something that I had to do to brighten the room up and keep the ginger off my back. Almost anyone who knew Tom had worked for him at some time or another. Whether it was laying floors, digging up floors, or driving a van, we all needed the extra money, and I was no exception.

At that time, I was part of a crew that was tearing up old lino floors in a large building in Basingstoke. While working the evening shift, I picked up a roll of adhesive circles about six inches in diameter. I thought that they'd look fancy stuck to the plasterboard and spaced at symmetrical intervals. To my surprise, Tom did not seem too bothered when I began placing the circles in a pretty pattern. In fact, he was willing to be the first one to sign his name within one of the circles and add a comment. Like the king of the terrace, he held the brown marker and scrawled 'Tom the bomb' as if he had just endorsed the Magna Carta. His symbol of leadership stood out like a beacon of hope in the middle of the clean white discs and started a mad scramble for those keen to be a part of this piece of history. The nineteen remaining circles were taken up instantly by Jesse Terrace inhabitants and the customary visitors. It was an honour to be assigned a circle on the wall. Over the next few months, aspiring artists and piss artists were to fill in the gaps between the circles with some wise idioms and satirical sketches.

It would not be long before all existing grey space on the plasterboard wall was completely taken, thus creating a masterly work of art. Some of my favourite characters to grace this tapestry included King Kat Water Wet Melon Man, Hazel Bites the Toilet, the Sinogliserus (a small hand-shaped character with a large rubber stopper nose), the Big Red Rock Eater, and who could forget the formidable Army in the Mouthy?

The wall's reputation took on a life of its own. More than once, I returned from work to find complete strangers socialising in my room, and when I asked them why they were trespassing on the premises, it was always the same reply: 'We're here to read the wall.' If only I had charged an entrance fee!

CHAPTER 14

LILY BROWN'S, REBECCA'S, AND BIGGLES

For years, Reading had not a lot to offer in the way of extracurricular activities as far as night clubs were concerned, and the ones it did have had a few drawbacks. The Top Rank was too big, Bones was too small, and the Caribbean Club had too much kid curry. I was quite impressed with the size of the Top Rank, but the lack of atmosphere and people in such a big place made it feel cold.

My first visit to the Top Rank was at the invite of someone whom I had briefly met a week before. I was introduced to Jimmy Maloney by Beaker in the Boars Head one afternoon during one of his lunch breaks. When Beaker went back to work, Jimmy and I had another pint. Then he asked if I'd like to accompany him in a spot of shopping. He said he was going to the Top Rank on that Saturday and that he needed a new outfit for the occasion. As my diary for the day had plenty of gaps, I agreed to tag along. He said that he needed new shoes and that he fancied a pair he'd previously seen in a shop in Chain Street facing Heelas. We entered said premises, and I was struck by how expensive everything was. Jimmy did not say what he did for a living, but I thought that he must have been well paid if he could afford anything from this particular shop. As I browsed the shelves of the pricey collection of cobbling fare, Jimmy was handling a fine pair of shoes at the front of the shop. I glanced back to see if he'd made his choice and realised that he was gone. I quickly gathered that the matter of money was irrelevant as he had quite clearly done a runner. I looked at the doors then back to the counter, where the young shop assistant was standing with her head bowed, reading a magazine and totally unaware of what had just occurred. One more look, and I was also gone as I didn't want to be implicated in the great shoe caper. Jimmy was nowhere to be seen.

Later that day, I did cross his path again, and by this time, he had a full a wardrobe consisting of new shirt, tie, trousers, and trench coat. He had a job, but on his days off, he was a tea leaf. Even though Jimmy had left me high and dry in the shoe shop in the midst of one of his moves, I thought it would be interesting to meet up with him on the Saturday. We became good friends; it would have been hard not to take to him with that perpetual glint in his eye and the mischievous grin. Later I also built up a friendship with his brother Mick despite embarrassing him at Prospect Park one Saturday afternoon. He ended up chasing shadows whilst trying to mark me when he played for the post office football team in local cup action. Even though he was a decent midfield player, he was out of his depth trying to curtail my impressive skills and was left in awe as I netted two superb goals in a 3–2 victory.

Biggles, another club that we occasionally went to, was also a great craic. It was located on the outskirts of town, four miles away, on an old aerodrome in Woodley. The only snag was that some form of transportation was needed to get there. It was there in 1931 that Pilot Officer Douglas Bader of the Royal Air Force caught the wingtip of his Bristol Bulldog on the ground when attempting a roll too low. Apparently, this exploit was only carried out after a colleague offered Douglas a wager during lunch, convinced that this stunt could not be done. He was partially correct as Mr Bader did roll but ended up entangled in a crumpled heap of twisted metal minus a couple of legs. He was close to death but recovered to rejoin the RAF and fight during the Second World War, where he lost some more legs.

Biggles had a swimming pool that was open to any drunkard that fancied a midnight dip, and surprisingly, as far as I know, everyone lived to tell the tale. Upon arrival, most people enjoyed a few beers or cocktails then boogied on down on the dance floor and rocked on their bums, rowing along to 'Oops Upside Your Head'. Aquatic time only seemed to come around at the end of the evening when everyone was blotto. A few brave/drunk girls stripped down to their bras and panties before taking the plunge, but the pool was mostly filled with scrawny intoxicated males. Although most of the clientele had had a few, there were not many patrons dopey enough to jump in fully clothed. On one occasion, a crowd of us carefully stacked our attire in a dry location and ensured that it was in a safe-enough distance away from splashing bombers. We all took the dip in our Y-fronts and were merrily having a fine old time until Mad Dog Rolfie decided to gather up all the clothing into his arms and join us in the pool. There was a scattering match as we frantically slapped about to grab the drifting bank notes that floated to the surface. It was wise to keep one eye on Rolfie at all times.

What these clubs lacked was the feeling of intimacy. The town needed somewhere one could be wined and dined in plush velvet seats and dimmed lighting to enjoy a romantic evening. A club called Lily Brown's opened in Caversham. It was a bit upmarket, and although it was trendier than other clubs, they found it difficult to fill the place. Maybe they would have had more success if they had not evicted and barred customers for trivial affairs, such as eating the plants that decorated the tables. The name was changed to Cavershams, and it soon became the most popular nightclub in town. It had everything: great music, beer, and comfortable surroundings. The fancy lounge at the back—the Doubles Bar—was the place to be. Although a bit more expensive, it kept the riff-raff out. There was little trouble in Cavershams, a place that welcomed all sorts, from Irish people to a six-foot-four transvestite who might or might not have been a scaffolder during the day.

Another club that opened around that time was Rebecca's. Located underground close to the train station, it was also a popular hangout when the pubs shut. It was not as relaxed as Cavershams; there was always an edgy feeling to the place. Security was tight, and they had a strict dress code and a low tolerance level from the bouncers if they perceived any kind of inappropriate behaviour. At some time or another,

I'd been barred from most drinking establishments, so it was not surprising when I got the heave-ho from Rebecca's.

In my defence, the punishment was a bit harsh when the alleged crime was that I was guilty of acting slovenly. At that time, I was unable to argue the point as I did not know what the word meant. As far as bans went, it was short and sweet, so it wouldn't be long before I was back in again, this time making sure that I was not so slovenly. Although the bouncers did a thorough body search for weapons and other illegal materials upon entering the club, they failed every time John went through the doors.

Around that time, an extremely large angry person was on the warpath and, for some reason, was out for John's blood. To counteract the possibility of an unprovoked attack, John thought that he should even the field a bit by carrying a sawn-off hammerhead in his pocket. Each time he was patted down at the entrance, he would simply put his hands in his jacket pocket and spread it open for a body search, all the while holding the hammerhead firmly in one hand. Using this deft tactic, he was able to hoodwink the heavies on numerous occasions. Fortunately, the weapon was never used; if it had been, the end result could have been fatal.

One particular evening, we again found ourselves back at our favourite rugby club. This time was to be my last at this venue as even I was appalled by the so-called entertainment that night. I'd been involved in very few altercations since arriving on the shores of the Thames, but one place seemed to be a magnet for unruly activities. This rugby club seemed to be operated by gentlemen and frequented by hooligans. One particular night saw the gathering of some of Reading's finest illiterates who were to take in a stag night which seemed to be open to anyone who could afford it. There was no wedding or groom attached to the event: it was just an organised booze-up to watch a few old slappers take their clothes off. For the really unlucky individual, the chance of being summoned to the stage for a shag was a distinct possibility, as was a dose of the clap. The place was bunged, and as per usual, the demon liquor converted the common slob within the audience into a drunken savage. Early evening banter would later progress into dangerous vitriol as the various tribes from each part of town puffed out their chests. Some of the rabid testosterone–laced Neanderthals were looking for a rumble, particularly a mob from Whitley. There were about ten of us from the Jesse Terrace crowd, and it seemed as if no one would take the bait being offered up by the antagonists. Unfortunately, Stef eventually couldn't help himself. He had been confronted by an overly intoxicated associate of the Whitley whiff as he was returning from a quick lash, and the both of them had to be separated by one of the staff members.

Towards the end of the night, the second-rate strippers began to bore the onlookers and were bombarded with shouts of 'Get them on!' That was the cue to step it up a notch, and they soon began to offer their horrible bodies to who ever wanted them. Within seconds, tables and chairs were flipped over, and bottles were scattered as a few punters scrambled to get to the stage, disrobing and slinging their clothing over their shoulders as they went. Roared on by the unruly mob, a few fat, sweaty, beer-bellied lager louts puffed and panted as they spread the blotchy thighs of the unsightly ladies of the night. Not a pretty sight. The bell for last orders rang and the copulating sideshow was broken up by staff members, who dragged the rabid oafs to their corners. As the different factions headed to the entrances, unease was in the air, and a lot of verbal abuse was flying. Before any disorder occurred, we rallied our flock for a quick escape.

Andy was the first to exit the premises, wobbling his head about and talking to John, who was following just behind. Now Andy was one of the most placid people in Berkshire and did not deserve the severe belt in the kisser that awaited him as he stepped through the doorway. He was dropped like a whore's drawers, totally oblivious to the thug standing in the shadows who had delivered the knuckle sandwich. Before Andy had hit the dirt, his attacker was also decked by an uppercut from John.

The mugger was easily twice John's weight but was taken out of action in an instant and was soon lying on the ground like a dead ant, mumbling at the moon. Then the free-for-all began. Skirmishes took place immediately as the different parties emerged from the main hall. People were battering each other all over the grounds of the rugby club as fists flew in the car park and throughout the playing fields. It was bedlam. The dim lights from the main building made it difficult to distinguish friend from foe.

In one instance, someone cried out into the night, 'Dave! Dave, stop! Stop! It's me—Pat. I'm on your side!'

Dave was on top of his friend, delivering a few tasty blows for some collateral damage. There was a scattering match when the constabulary arrived, but the result was definitely a victory for the boys from Jesse, with Andy (and Pat) being the only casualties. I was glad to see the back of that dump.

CHAPTER 15

SKATING FOR A FISH SUPPER

Eugene had returned from Northern Ireland after a year's hiatus and was sharing a flat above a shop on Kings Road. One day, Neil asked him if he'd like to go to Richmond for an ice skating folly along with Muff, Cheryl, Richard Downs, and I. He was up for it, so we headed to the station and boarded the train to Richmond. It promised to be an interesting adventure as Muff, Eugene, and I had never graced an ice rink before. The others, on the other hand, sounded off as if they were Olympic champions and made us feel like little kids on a day out.

From Richmond Station, we had to take a short bus ride over the bridge to the ice rink, which was located on the other side of the Thames. As we were not sure at which stop to disembark, we stood holding on to the pole at the open back entranceway on one of the famous old red Routemasters. The bus would stop only for awaiting roadside passengers or if the cord to ring the bell was pulled. Still confused about when to get off, Neil suddenly called out that the next stop was where the rink was. As the bus slowed, Cheryl realised he was wrong, and she held her arm out in an effort to warn the rest of us to hold steady. But it was too late for Richard. He had already taken the hazardous leap from the platform. It might have seemed that the bus was hardly moving, but in reality, it was probably ticking along at about ten miles per hour. Taking into account the added momentum of Richard's gangly frame as he touched down, the final velocity when he hit the pavement must have been close to twenty miles per hour.

What we then witnessed was an ad-libbed animated movie in slow motion starring Richard D. and his amazing rotating legs. It was similar to watching a wind-up toy race car that already has its wheels spinning before it is released to zoom across the living room carpet. He was travelling at his body's full potential capacity, and as he ran, he arched ever closer to the ground until his nose was almost scraping the footpath. Miraculously, he started to gain control as he fought against the aerodynamic forces at play and pulled himself out of a crash landing. We had somehow managed to hang on to the bus pole even though we were doubled up in fits of side-splitting laughter. As he pulled his frame upright and away from the danger area, a dry smile lit up his face as he glanced in approval to his incredulous peers.

The event happened in a split second but seemed just like a film that had been slowed down. Although he'd regained control, he was still travelling at about ten miles per hour faster than his body could handle. It was then that the smug grin disappeared and was replaced with a look of shock and dismay. He'd taken his eye off the ball, and before he could begin the deceleration procedure, there was a direct hit with a rubbish bin. Wastepaper, bottles, and other soiled items were sent airborne, mixing with the blood and snotters from Richard's neb, which had been bashed in good and proper. The amusing show was momentarily put on hold when we exited the bus at the next stop. We were slightly concerned about the well-being of our skydiving pal, and we rushed back to the point of the premature spacewalk. When we found him, he was whistling Dixie and barely mobile, staggering like a drunken sailor. He seemed coherent, though it was difficult to analyse his condition as his normal state had been defective before the altercation with the rubbish bin.

Richmond ice rink was a very busy arena, and although over thirty miles away from where we lived, it was the closest place to the Reading area where one could strap on a set of blades. It was a given that the skating lark was going to be a challenge for the usual suspects: Muff, Eugene, and I. What we hadn't taken into account was that we would have to balance on ten-inch blades and negotiate an assault course filled with snivelling snotty-nosed brats kicking and biting their way to the ice. Standing up in a pair of skates was hard enough; but by the time we'd dragged ourselves along an endless corridor and down a rickety old flight of stairs, we were knackered, and our ankles were shot. Neil and Cheryl had already scooted across the ice like Torvill and Dean doing pirouettes to the imaginary sound of *Ravel's Bolero*. Richard, on the other hand, had decided to give the old slippery surface a miss to become a spectator after his dance with the devil.

Then the three stooges took to the ice. I went first, tentatively lifting my skate and placing it firmly on to the surface, but as I swung my other leg around to make complete contact, I face-planted into the slush. Muff and Eugene seemed to find my actions hilarious as they watched me slip and slither like a jellied eel. They then followed my lead—and copied my every move, including the face plant. When we did regain our footing, we hit the deck again as fast as we'd stood upright. It seemed highly unlikely that we could master the art of standing on skates, and it became almost impossible to do when inflicted with uncontrollable laughter. Then to my amazement, I was able to stand up like an authentic skater and move forward without folding. It was slow, but it was progress. As I eased my way across the ice, I glanced over my shoulder to see Pinky and Perky snorting and grunting as they kept hitting the deck and then pulling themselves up again by grabbing the arena boards. They were having a ball rolling around, and they were still laughing hysterically.

By the time they had mastered standing on the ice, I had graduated to cruising and weaving, feeling like I was the lord of the dance. Every now and again, Cheryl and Neil would blow by then skid to a halt, showering me with icy splinters. Muff, in due course, followed my lead and inched along away from the edge, but he was now in control. Then Eugene made the grade and built up a bit of momentum as he began to move as gracefully as Bambi in quicksand. He had spat in the face of adversity and began to cruise awkwardly, sporting a grin of self-satisfaction as he called out, 'Look at me. I can skate!'

He was indeed correct; he could skate, and he began to steadily increase his tempo. What this novice speed skater had not taken into consideration was how to initiate the art of stopping. His smug triumphant look was replaced with fear as he contemplated an imminent collision with the boards. Then *crunch!* Eugene thumped into the wooden wall and somersaulted gracefully to land amongst the sparsely scattered spectators. He lay groaning in a crumpled mess, clutching one of his knees. We skated over to check out the severity of our recently airborne friend's injury. One thing was certain: he would not add to his ten minutes of elegance on ice. It definitely was a day of collisions. The outing was now well and truly done, and we assisted our two wounded warriors back to Reading. Apparently, Eugene's injury to his knee was extreme, or so he let everyone believe it to be.

Now unfit to work, he was trapped in an upstairs flat, unable to negotiate the steep staircase that was the gateway to the front door. Feeling somewhat sorry for the poor soul, I phoned him one day to see if he'd like me to bring him some fish and chips round during my lunch break. Of course, he didn't say no. What I didn't take into account nor was I told by the lame tenant was that because of his defective knee, he was unable to reach the door to unlock it. When I arrived at the front of the premises, the famished detainee was shuffling about in the upstairs living room.

I called up, 'How am I goin' to get in?'

'Go around the back. There's a big set of doors on this level that I can open,' he replied.

So off I trotted with two fish suppers in hand to a small car park at the rear of the building. Eugene was standing by what looked like an old unloading entranceway and had opened one of the two large doors. It was all fine and dandy that he'd managed to let some fresh air into the smelly flat, but the pointless doorway led directly to a ten-foot drop and sudden death.

Baffled, I scratched my head and then asked, 'How am I supposed to get up there?'

'Climb up on to the ledge,' he answered. A small two-foot projection skirted the building, stopping just before the doorway.

'Are you mental? I'll probably kill myself,' I said.

'Well, it's the only way in,' he replied.

So like a mug, I fell for it. A van was strategically parked close to the wall of the building, a perfect location to establish a base camp. The waft of salt and vinegar from the lunch packages was creating severe hunger pains in my stomach. I climbed on to the ledge above and scuttled along, clutching the appetising snacks. With my back to the wall, I cautiously inched from side to side, edging closer to the windows as I prepared to hand the food to Eugene.

Before I could make the move, I saw a Jaguar XJS slide into the car park and stop close to the van below. A stylish middle-aged blonde exited the car. She revealed plenty of leg when her short skirt hiked up, exposing some fine black stockings and a pair of bare thighs.

A very tasty bit of stuff, I thought.

She seemed somewhat confused by the sight of a person in blue overalls perched precariously on a thin ledge halfway up a building with two fish suppers under his arm.

Staring directly at me, she asked, 'What are you doing climbing all over my property?'

'Nothin',' I answered.

'What do you mean nothing? You are on my building for some reason!' she exclaimed.

I was stuck like a deer in headlights and was struggling for a reply.

'Having lunch?' I squeaked.

She did not like my response. As I glanced to my left, I could hear the latch bolt being engaged as the large windows were slowly drawn shut. That was followed by the sound of a dull thump and a cackle akin to that of a demented hyena. The mysterious noise was in fact Eugene falling about laughing on the living room floor. Sheepishly, I climbed down from the building after the pretty lady in black stockings began snarling threats of police action in my general direction. The echoes of incessant roars of hilarity from Old Busted Knee could still be heard as I skulked out of the car park, with the elegant but enraged lady barking reprimands as I passed by. Eugene certainly enjoyed the show, but he was still hungry. I, on the other hand, made myself sick by gorging on a couple of fish suppers in the grounds of Forbury Gardens.

Fish seemed to be a topical subject at that time. Jesse Terrace welcomed a new tenant when Fish moved in and took up Simon's position. The place was now pretty much settled, with each of us adding our own piece of individuality to the scene. Tom was in control of the main floor, and we stayed well clear of the headquarters unless we were officially invited in. As far as the rest of us were concerned, the rooms were open for business, and we felt comfortable strolling about the house, infiltrating each other's personal space.

Jesse Terrace was a big house and had plenty of room to sleep five people. There were a lot of would-be contenders attempting to call this famous abode their own, but it was a closed shop. That would later change though, following a committee meeting and an in-house agreement to let someone else stay on a temporary basis. Eugene was soon to be out on his arse when his time was up where he was presently staying. He had been given the cold shoulder from various parties when sniffing around for some short-term accommodation. Being the gentleman that I was, I offered him my floor for a few weeks until he got back on his feet.

With Tom's approval, we picked up a mattress and squeezed it into the available space. Eugene's arrival solved an immediate dilemma for me as well. I'd been mulling over whether I should spend some much-needed beer and food money on a new pair of shoes. It had been less than four months since I'd last purchased what I thought was a decent pair, but the substandard stitching on my right shoe had split, leaving my toes flapping in the wind. I'd held back on slinging them because the left one was in mint condition, but wearing only one shoe was not a realistic solution. Enter Eugene, who was unaware that he had the answer to this enigma. I clocked his feet to see that he was wearing the exact same colour and make of shoes as mine, but I detected that he was also not too comfortable with the situation.

Lo and behold, the stitching on his left shoe was shot, leaving an untarnished right shoe and a very frustrated man from Kilkeel with a conundrum on par with mine. There was only going to be one satisfied punter to emerge from this cobbling disaster, and that was me. Eugene's plates of meat were a size larger than mine, so regrettably for him, he had to discard his beloved footwear, whereas I—having the smaller feet—was able to nab his good right shoe for a matching pair. So off I plodded with a new pair of shoes, albeit one of them a different size than the other.

Getting used to being in each other's faces wasn't much of a problem as we did most things together after work and on weekends. Not so much at the beginning of the day though. Eugene got a job as a carpenter and had an early start, but it also meant that I would never be able to sleep in again. Before he moved in, I had usually lazed around, rising from my slumber by 7.30 a.m., but that soon changed. Each morning, the annoying shrill of his alarm went off at 6 a.m., but did he wake up? No chance. He would be still in the land of Nod, snoring away like a broken chainsaw and oblivious to the racket that was occurring; eventually, I had to get up and yell into his lug in an effort to rouse him. I would then crawl back into bed to try to regain some of my stolen sleep. Also, as he tried to dress for work in the darkened room, I would usually get a big toe stuffed up my nose or one of his sweaty feet planted across my jawbone as he headed for the bathroom.

Weekends tended to be more problematic when negotiating the bedroom's four walls after a skin full of lager. On one such night, after ten pints and a curry, I'd gone to sleep with a piece of leftover chicken from my tandoori mixed grill placed conveniently beside the bed for breakfast. In the middle of the night, I was rudely awakened by Eugene doing a full-body slam on top of me after skidding on my tasty bedside morsel. His long spider monkey toes had reached out to grasp the chicken quarter marinated in red curry sauce as he staggered to find his way to the toilet. I had to carefully dust off his DNA from the breakfast fare before consuming it the next morning. You must have breakfast; it's the most important meal of the day.

Word got around of an upcoming fancy dress party that was occurring in Caversham. One of our crowd had been invited, so that was good enough for the rest of us to attend. As others contemplated what costume they should wear, a few of us had already decided that we should all go as Alfie Keys. Alfie was a right plonker who had recently surfaced in the Boars Head; he exhibited a unique skill of boring people to death. He was an ugly bastard without doubt who sported an unkempt black beard and who was perpetually dressed in blue jeans topped by a red T-shirt. Although his first name was in fact Alfie, the surname Keys was bestowed upon him because he was first and foremost a right plonker. He would prance about the bar with an air of superiority as for some unknown reason he had convinced himself that the absurd number of dangling keys bunched together and clipped to his belt made him better than everyone else. So four red T-shirts later and after a trip to the joke shop for some false beards along with a black hair dye rinse, we were ready to transform into Alfie Keys. The dye was supposed to wash out within a few days. My silky black hair colouring did not in fact wash out for two weeks and gradually evolved into a fancy shade of royal blue. This in turn caused me to endure endless taunts and wolf whistles from my co-workers on the building site.

Muff had been collecting keys for the occasion and had a chain-linked assortment hanging from his belt that almost touched the ground. I went to Mothercare and purchased a bundle of plastic keys that were used to help babies with teething problems. Gus twisted a lump of copper wire to his belt and hung a few pots and pans from it, making a right racket when he walked along. The red T-shirts were no problem, but we did struggle somewhat when sticking our beards on. Finally, we were ready, and the three Alfie Keys clones headed out for a quick pint before going on to the party. Fish was supposed to be the fourth Alfie, but he had to work late that night and started yapping when he eventually got home and found that someone had stolen his beard. First stop was the Travellers Friend in Friar Street. It was not the prettiest pub in Reading, and our reception by the red-faced navvies was not unexpected.

'And who are you supposed to be—the three bearded pansies?' one of them asked.

Gus strolled over to confront the drunken manual worker, yelling into his face, 'Fuck off!' He banged two of his pots together in front of the bloke's face, causing the poor chap to flee in fear for his life.

131

One pint there would suffice. We entertained and confused a few people in a couple of other pubs en route to the venue. When we arrived at the party, our resemblance to the real Alfie Keys had diminished as various parts of our props had fallen off along the way. We did make an effort to hang out with Alfie for part of the night, but it was lost on the star of the show as the dopey bastard never clued into the fact that we were meant to be him. Maybe it was because for the first time in his life he wore a *yellow* T-shirt that night.

Although we went full out at the weekends, most of us put in a hard day's graft from Monday to Friday. At the end of one such long five-day slog, I remember Eugene suggesting that we should go down the Butler and sit on the bar stools and drink until we fell off them. And that we did do. Another weekend, we thought that instead of doing the same old thing, we should try going to a different pub instead. As it happened, it was not a good idea, particularly for me. Muff, Gus, Eugene, and I headed down to Coopers Wine Bar for a change, and although the name suggests a tasty little upmarket retreat, it was in fact a shithole full of squaddies and old slappers looking for a shag from a soldier.

We hadn't been in there long, standing at the bar and having a tipple, when two unpredictable characters, Willie and Webby, burst through the front doors and joined our company. They were well known to us and likeable enough but were pests likely to end up in some sort of hassle. Their semi-punk dress style—Webby with spiked blonde hair and undersized clothes and Willie with his black spiked hair, mascara-lined eyes, and gothic attire—made them easily recognizable.

Oftentimes during a pint with us, Willie might look at his watch and explain, 'Oh, I have to go now. I've got a fight in half an hour.' Then he would go off and invariably get his bollocks knocked in.

On this particular night, they were breathing heavily and seemed quite perturbed.

'What's up with you two?' I asked.

We usually believed Willie's patter as he was from London and reasonably smart, whereas Webby was as thick as two short planks and from up north.

'We've got ourselves into a bit of bother and wondered if you'd back us up when we leave,' said Willie.

'What bother?' said Gus.

'I think there'll be a few fellas waiting on us outside, but they'll do nothing if you're with us,' he said.

'How many?' I asked.

'About four of five,' Willie replied.

We looked at each other and nodded in approval, agreeing that we should accompany our two twitchy friends upon leaving. After downing our pints, it was time to make a move. Like a mug, I exited first and saw at least twenty people crowded around the doorway; on my next step, I took a bottle directly to the head and went crashing to the ground. The last thing I remember was seeing Willie running in one direction, being chased by half of the group, and Webby whizzing away in the other direction with the remainder in hot pursuit. My next recollection was standing over a sink in the toilets, with Eugene picking bits of broken bottle from my scalp and pouring cold water on the wound. So later it was off to the hospital for yet more stitches. My head was now like a British rail train map. That's what you get when you assist crazies.

In contrast, our household activities tended to be rather subdued during the week. Tom had a television, but he liked his privacy, and the only person with a free pass to his room was his new girlfriend, Hazel. Later, this unassuming little lady would move in with Tom, and they would subsequently have a baby boy together. Because of this, the rest of us were usually sprawled around my room, watching an old beat-up black-and-white TV that I'd picked up for a couple of quid at the second-hand shop. The picture was grainy at the best of times, and every now and again, it would disappear completely. But it could be easily recovered by a forceful stamp on the floor. We used this method to rectify the situation often; eventually our feet would hit the floor instinctively, resulting in a foot-stomping ensemble banging on the floor in unison as we attempted to recover the picture. It sounded like a very well-drilled army patrol standing to attention.

A programme then that we never missed was *Minder*, and we'd get prepared for it with a cup of tea and biscuits. The tea maker was the one who answered the least amount of questions correctly on *University Challenge*: a must-watch show for the seasoned intellectual upper-class twat. It was on immediately before *Minder* and was hosted by the inflatable-headed Bamber Gascoigne. If any of us managed to get one answer right, then it would be safe to say that someone else was to make the tea. If we weren't gathered around, watching telly, we would play the state-of-the art trailblazing Atari tennis video game.

Eugene and I were accustomed to the odd trip to the cinema from time to time to watch any old shit or just for something to do. On one occasion, we found ourselves slightly out of our depth during the original showing of the Sex Pistols' *The Great Rock 'n' Roll Swindle*. Swarms of extravagantly dressed eccentrics had congregated outside the Odeon in Cheap Street and encircled the two seasoned movie buffs. Although clad in denim, we gave off an appearance of a couple of civil servants amongst the rabid band of intimidating punks. Their image was deceiving as most of the threatening-looking individuals were in fact good lads or lasses. If we did go the pub during the week, it would only be for a swift pint as there was no life in the town until Thursday or Friday. Other larks included in-house Formula One racing as we battled it out on a Scalextrix set that Simon had nabbed from his younger brothers, twins Tim and Nick. The track circumnavigated the room, with chicanes weaving under the piano then straightening out between the beds. Finally, the cars that managed to stay on the track screeched to the finishing line at the portable Calor gas fire.

When we were really bored, some strange occurrences took place in the kitchen, including pitch and toss, shove halfpenny games, and unusual ways to butter toast. After grilling up some crusty slices, I buttered a piece with my elbow, Eugene used his nose, and Gus spread it sparingly with the leg of a chair. I don't recall if we ate the toast; maybe Muff did after a poke about in the bin. Another time, we became a bit more theatrical when Muff got his hands on a recording system with two microphones. We used the equipment to act out an audio play that I had previously attempted to pen, called *The Mystery of the Missing Maisonette*. Muff used various sound effects between the microphones to portray a desperate man hurrying into his room to have a stiff drink and a strong cigar.

He'd run on the spot, pour water into a glass from a height, and strike matches to set the scene for the listener, and then say, 'Henri Winterman's, I presume?'

Muff was outstanding in the lead role of the worried Tommy of the Top Floor with supporting cast members Gordon of the Ground Floor (played by Eugene) and Malcolm of the Middle Floor (played by yours truly). The protagonist and his sidekicks were grilled about the mystery of the missing maisonette by the incomparable Inspector Skelf and his assistant PC Throat. The drama was about the bizarre disappearance of the dwelling next to the three friends, and although the play was never completed, we did have a hilarious time acting it out.

When we were low on cash, most of us would find a bit of work on the side in some capacity; usually it was helping Tom, but we sometimes found our own jobs. Muff, Eugene, and a fellow called Jeff managed to pick up a nice little earner decorating a detached house in Sonning Common owned by an attractive lady. With the possibility of further jobs to come, they were keen to do good work, so proper preparation of the wooden window frames before painting was essential. Muff drew the short straw and was to work up a ladder on the outside of the upstairs windows; Jeff and Eugene got to do the cushy bit on the inside of the frames. They started on the master bedroom, which was used by the lady of the house. Muff positioned the ladder, ensuring it was safely anchored as he was concerned that a sudden jolt of any kind could make him lose his balance. He was happy at his work, humming a merry tune as he scraped away contently. Jeff was preparing to do the same inside the house, and Muff could hear him shuffling around on the other side of the window. He could not see in because of the heavy drawn curtains. Minutes later, Muff almost fell to his death when the curtains were pulled back to reveal his near-naked co-worker Jeff standing with his legs spread provocatively, wearing only a black bra, panties, stockings, and suspenders. Instead of preparing to undress the window frame of loose paint particles, he had undressed himself of his work clothing. He had rifled through the host's underwear drawer so that he could provide Muff with a shocking sideshow.

Another Reading Festival was upon us, and it brought with it thousands of wandering minstrels who set up camp for a few days along the banks of the Thames. I'd never paid for a ticket before, always having gained entrance by climbing the fence or tunnelling under it. This year was not going to be as easy as security was tighter, with guards dressed like the Gestapo patrolling the grounds. Slade and particularly Rod Stewart were two of the bill toppers, hence the extra police contingent. Neil's girlfriend, Tracy, and her pal Sue had managed to get hired helping out backstage, which meant they'd be rubbing shoulders with all the top acts.

Backstage was the dream place to be. It was an intricate tent village complete with neon signs which illuminated the restaurants, bars, and coffee shops that had been set up to pamper the rich and famous. Tracy and Sue had a plan to get us backstage. They were to exit security, carrying a pass borrowed from a male associate, then return with whoever was around at the time. The pass had no photo ID to prove ownership, so it would be a breeze. Neil, Eugene, and I were the chosen three to hit the big time. Tracy successfully took Neil on a trial run through Check Point Charlie. Then Eugene won the coin toss to see who would follow. We had to move away from the gates as it took quite a while for Tracy to return with the pass, and the staff members were giving us the evil eye as our loitering did look somewhat suspicious. Eugene had been inside for over thirty minutes before it was my turn to mingle with the elite. I had been pacing around the fence perimeter, trying to lie low, but it was well worth the wait.

As I entered tent city, Rod Stewart and the beautiful Britt Ekland sailed past me on their way to one of the bars. I made a quick left turn and was hot on their heels, hoping to have a sniff of Britt. They ducked under a canvas gateway and into a fancy bar, but just as I lowered my head to follow, an extremely large grunter thrust his shovel-like hand into my face and politely told me to beat it. This area was out of bounds for the minions. In my haste to be part of Rod's entourage, I'd lost

Tracy, and I was now without a pass, which meant my time backstage could have been limited.

Fortunately, I was able to locate the others; they seemed to be having a fine time in a large open bar where they were socialising with some of the headliners. Tracy and Sue were conversing with Noddy Holder and Jimmy Lea from Slade, but I could not locate Neil or Eugene. Tracy nonchalantly pointed her finger to the back of the tent. They were sitting on the floor, leaning comfortably back into the tent wall and swigging a beer, and they had their arms wrapped around someone in the middle. They seemed to be having a ball as they laughed and joked with this unknown person. As I got closer, I realised that their new best mate was Rory Gallagher. Keen to be part of this joviality, I rushed to the bar to grab a bottle and made haste to join in the camaraderie. Just as I was about to indulge in a bit of banter with my old mate Rory, he was up on his heels as he bid adieu to his new friends. I stood motionless with my jaw open, catching flies, knowing that I'd missed out on spending some quality time a with a guitar legend.

Quite a few girls were peripheral to our group; some of them eager to establish themselves as part of the Jesse Terrace scene. If they chose to take the initiative and approach one of us for a good time, then it would have to be done early, or they would risk being lumbered with a drunken, babbling idiot by the end of the night. That was generally the case as it was rare to leave the bar when the pints were flowing and the chit-chat was jovial. On one such night, Eugene whispered into my lug that he had been chatting up a bit of stuff and was possibly on for the ride and that she had a mate that fancied me. I glanced over to see a tasty pair of ladies; if they were willing, then it was definitely worth breaking our policy about leaving the pub early. They agreed to come back to Jesse Terrace with us as long as we didn't push our luck, so we promised to be good boys. We knew that they'd soon melt to our Ulster charm and we would easily be able to climb on, but then I thought about how messy our room was.

Something had to be done swiftly, so I said to Eugene, 'The room's a tip, and the mattress on the floor looks like it's set up for a shagging match. They'll take one look and clear aff.'

137

'You're right. I'll run back and hide it somewhere. Keep them talking. Give me twenty minutes. Tell them I've gone for a carry-out, then bring them round,' he said with his mind working overtime.

After some idle banter, I waltzed from the pub with the ladies in tow. I was giving it some old chat, trying to impress them with a load of old bollocks, but it was obvious they had no idea what I was saying or what planet I was from. Upon arrival, I discovered that Eugene had the room tidied and the lights down low; the curtains had been strategically drawn, creating an ambience of love. Soothing music emanated from my digital alarm clock radio. Eugene poured the girls a glass of the finest Blue Nun, and then we settled down beside our respective partners, edging ever closer as we hoped for a positive reaction. I had successfully managed to snake an arm around the waist of my significant other without any protest and was about to take an extra step by nuzzling her earlobe. This move was uncharted territory and could either have been a stimulating erotic experience for the little lady or could have resulted in her receiving a lug full of saliva. Eugene was also cracking on like a well-oiled machine as he used his enlarged nasal glands to sniff various regions of his date's fragrant neck.

Everything was going well, and the girls were responding positively to our tender posturing. Alas, our passionate playmaking was about to come crashing to the ground when the full-length curtains that covered the French windows began to flutter slightly. Seconds later, the grubby old mattress that Eugene had ingeniously hidden made a grand entrance by falling from behind the curtains that parted like the Red Sea. Before the dust could settle, our pair of lovebirds concluded that this room full of beds was not for them. Maybe they thought it was the sign that some perverted satanic hanky-panky was about to begin. They grabbed their bags and legged it down the road, never to be seen again.

Eugene shrugged his shoulders and said, 'We might as well go back down the pub!'

So we strolled down Howard Street towards the town centre and went back into the Boars Head without anyone noticing that we'd been gone.

CHAPTER 16

THREE IN A BED IN PARIS

John Lennon's recent tragic death saw his songs 'Imagine' and 'Woman' top the charts at the end of 1980, with 'In the Air Tonight'—perhaps dedicated to a Phil Collins fart—close behind. The first few months of the new year saw some startling headlines and a couple that made you shake your head. The notorious Yorkshire Ripper (Peter Sutcliffe, a thirty-five-year-old lorry driver from Bradford) was charged with the murders of thirteen women, Prince Charles and Lady Di got engaged, and Bucks Fizz won the Eurovision Song Contest with 'Making Your Mind Up'. Also, an extremely learned twat—the Archbishop of Canterbury—cleared up the situation concerning gay people by advising the church to see homosexuality as a handicap and not a sin. In football action, Aston Villa struggled to defend their first championship title in seventy-one years. Perhaps the three-points-for-a-win rule that had been introduced confused them; besides, Liverpool was again the strongest team.

Additionally, I'd missed out on a great double from the bookies that year. I'm sure that Ladbrokes would have offered me some great odds on the new president of the United States and the pope both being assassinated in quick succession. Ronald Reagan became the fortieth US president, succeeding Jimmy Carter, and within four months, he and Pope John Paul II would be shot. Had I bet on the two of them getting killed, I wouldn't have received the money as both of them eventually made full recoveries.

Easter was again upon us, and Simon asked if I fancied going on a trip to Paris. It seemed to be a great idea, so I was immediately on board. Gus and Eugene were also up for it and an unexpected extra—Stuart—decided to throw his hat into an adventure to the unknown. This was to be a relaxed cultural tour of the City of Lights and a means to bring out and enrich our artistic sides. It had to be that way as the previous journey to Amsterdam the year before had nearly killed us off. The Paris outing, on the other hand, had to be a mellow one. Our plan was to drive to Victoria Station and leave the car there before taking the train to Brighton. There we would board the hydrofoil bound for Calais, then head to Paris, and see what happened next.

We left Reading at five in the morning and cruised down the M4 in my 1966 maroon Ford Zepyhr; I'd recently bought it from Tom, and now I was finally going somewhere in it. With virtually no cars on the motorway, the shadowy red glow on the horizon at sunrise gave the early morning drive a paranormal feeling. The introduction of an oversized joint added a further spaced-out experience as Simon and Stuart busily began rolling their quota for the trip. Gus and Eugene were happily in the land of Nod. We left the Zephyr in a multistorey car park and then boarded the train.

Upon reaching our port of call, the second-hand smoke from the super joints began to take its toll on a liberal non-smoker such as myself. I seemed to be the only one who was stoned. None of us had ever been on a sea jet before, and we prepared ourselves for a rapid crossing. It was an interesting departure. The captain summoned all on board to fasten their seat belts; then the large craft's engines roared as it hovered just above the rough waves as it prepared to scoot across the channel. Instead of the expected forward thrust, however, the engines ceased, and we dropped like a stone and splashed into the water.

Then the captain made an announcement. 'I'm sorry for the discomfort, but we seem to be having a technical problem.'

For the next hour, we went nowhere, apart from bobbing about on the surf like plastic ducks in a bath. In due course, we zoomed away to

France after the repairs had been carried out. The four days spent in the French capital had a little bit of everything. Stuart recognised the name Montmartre on the map, so we made our way to the Metro to catch a train on the expansive underground system. Simon was keen to use his high school French but could not remember any of it. After a crash course for dummies from the rest of us, he was ready to order five tickets.

He walked up to the kiosk, repeating, 'Cinq billet, cinq billet, cinq billet.'

When he reached the booth, he leaned forward and confidently requested, 'Sank tickets!'

It was lucky there weren't six of us.

Upon arrival in the arty-farty Montmartre area, we found a small hotel that only had three available rooms. Gus was quick to grab the lone single. Simon and I then took the room with twin beds, leaving Eugene and Stuart to share a cosy double bed. After a quick pit stop, we were all set to explore the city. We cruised the Left Bank, immersing ourselves in the Gallic culture with visits to the Louvre, Pompidou Museum, Moulin Rouge, and a quick shufti over the rooftops from the Eiffel Tower's summit. Our love affair with the city was enhanced by a few little pick-me-ups as we navigated the Parisian walkways, as depicted by Gary Moore.

Dotted amongst these mellow moments were periods of chaos. Eugene, Gus, and I somehow got into a scrap in a crowded street with a gang of bizarre high-haired Oriental gentlemen. Allegedly, Eugene and I had been on top of some car roofs on opposite sides of the street, which would have been fine if some of them hadn't belonged to the triads. The next night, Simon and I touched for a couple of English lasses. I ended up in Port Orleans, a southerly suburb of Paris, only to be snubbed at the hotel door by my true love. I spent the next hour or so wandering past shifty-looking characters huddled around burning braziers as I negotiated my way through shady Algerian ghettos. Then I became tangled in the web of the Metro boarding trains that snaked through tunnels to destinations unknown.

When I finally remembered where the nearest station to the hotel was, Simon would not let me into the room as he was shacked up with the bit of stuff he'd pulled. She was howling at the moon, begging Simon to try to meet her sexual desires. I could hear her demanding more as the rabid couple exchanged a series of worrisome guttural groans.

'Hurt me. Hurt me, Simon! Give me nine inches and hurt me.'

So he offered her a baguette, ridiculed her hairstyle, and advised her that her dress sense was slightly dated. There was no chance of me breaking that disturbing scene up, so I shuffled over to see if I could rouse Gus; it was all to no avail as he was out for the count. My last chance of getting forty winks was to wake Eugene or Stuart, and after about ten minutes of constant banging on the door, a bleary-eyed Eugene finally let me in.

'You're sleeping on the floor,' he groaned then climbed back into bed.

I lay down on the cold ceramic tiles, but there would be no chance of me getting to sleep in such uncomfortable circumstances. I stood up to see Eugene and Stuart barely hanging on to the edges of the bed, obviously ill at ease about any of their body parts touching. There was a gap in the middle of the bed wide enough to drive a double-decker bus through, so I leaped into the inviting spot between them and clocked out.

The next morning, the three of us were awakened by a shaft of sunlight beaming through the small window on a fine Paris morning. Eugene and Stuart were both puzzled as to why they had a sprinkling of blood on various parts of their bodies. I had inadvertently bled on them from a gushing head wound that I had most likely sustained whilst re-enacting my role as phantom of the Metro the previous night. We cleaned up and met with Gus in the hallway as we waited for Simon to raise his head after his bout of lovemaking.

The door finally swung open, forcing the four of us to gasp and step back in anguish when we came face-to-face with Simon's northern belle. She was without a doubt the ugliest girl that we had ever seen. But love is blind, or at least Simon was, as he nodded and took the little lady, whom we would later affectionately call the Carlisle Pig, away for breakfast.

After a concluding stroll along the Champs-Élysées and a few group snapshots, we bade Paris a final adieu as we headed back to old Blighty.

I had no money before Paris and even less upon returning, but it didn't stop me from spending the next weekend in the Republic of Ireland. Stef's girlfriend, Antoinette (Paddy), had decided it was time for him to meet her family, so she organised a trip to Dublin. Muff; his partner, Cheryl; and her friend Lorna, a girl that I was seeing from time to time, were also invited. Someone suggested that I should come along to make up the numbers. Apart from being penniless, I was knackered following the escapades in Paris and really needed a break from all the recent overindulging. After minimal objection, I was coaxed into joining the others, with Stef slipping me some readies for a temporary loan. Besides, if Antoinette's family was anything like she was, then the craic would surely be great. Stef had rented a Ford Cortina estate car that seated only five people, so I was shoved into the back along with the luggage. The two-and-a-half-hour drive to Wales left me with a sore back as I endured the bumpy ride in steerage class before boarding the ferry. Stef was like the dad of a family on tour, constantly scolding Muff and me for bouncing objects off the back of his nut while he was driving.

Crossing the Irish Sea was rough, but I had previously earned my sea legs when working in the galley of the Larne-Stranraer boat, installing a dumbwaiter. It also helped that the Guinness on board this Dublin-bound craft was splendid. The art of Guinness pouring in England was equivalent to that of a load of Irish drunks attempting the hankie-waving Morris dance. My first and last pint in Reading came when a barman offered me a pint of slops from an electric pump that was poured in a matter of seconds. It was pure sacrilege that these uneducated brewers could do so much damage to the finest export that Ireland has ever produced. Not so on the ferry though, and as we sailed the Irish Sea, each drink slid down my neck with little resistance.

Six hours or so later, the boat docked. The weather was typical, with sheets of rain battering the gangplank as we disembarked. I hadn't been to Dublin since the Troubles began, and I was a bit wary of how a Belfast Protestant would be received in the fine city. The Guinness had helped to reduce my anxiety. My worrying turned out to be all in vain as Antoinette's hospitable family gave us a warm reception upon arrival. Apart from the fact that they were all Celtic supporters, they seemed OK. I did get a bit of a fright though when one large chap halted our progress to single me out.

'Which one of you is the fella from Belfast?' he enquired.

'That would be me,' I answered hesitantly.

'Are you the eejit with one shoe bigger than the other?' he asked with a snigger.

Word of my fabled mismatched feet had somehow filtered across the Irish Sea, making me a bit of a celebrity in that part of the Emerald Isle. So happily I obliged by putting my best foot forward and brandishing Eugene's old size 9 shoe, proudly displaying it with my old size 8 original. This little sideshow was a good way to break the ice at any party.

Nothing exciting happened during the long weekend. The one day it didn't rain, and we did a bit of sightseeing when our 'dad,' Stef, took us to the beautiful Glendalough Park in the Wicklow Mountains. There we snapped a few photos and ambled merrily on the hillside. The rest of the time, we were in the pub. A strange happening took place in Dublin's city centre as we settled in for a pint at a cosy tavern around lunchtime. One of us—probably not me—had just paid for some beers when we noticed the other patrons coming back from the bar, each with a tray load of pints. At first, I thought they were all just greedy bastards, but then the pub man rang a bell and shouted last orders. It was just approaching the noon hour so what was going on? Apparently, we had entered some type of time warp through a portal controlled by the pope. Because the pub was situated within a mile of a special chapel, no drinks could be served during the 'holy hour'. You could still drink beer, but none could be purchased. The smart locals had stocked up before the bell, leaving the tourists high and dry.

Alas, all things must pass, and we had to say goodbye to our hosts and the magnificent Guinness and pubs in the city of Dublin. The trip back was miserable, with passengers throwing up all over the deck as the ferry rose and fell under the constant attack from the vicious waves of the Irish Sea. Back on dry land, our fatigued group slumped into the Cortina for a long and tedious trek back to Reading. On the whole, it was a subdued drive, with the silence intermittently broken by an odd watery fart and one of the girls exclaiming, 'That is disgusting!' We arrived back at Jesse Terrace late that night, and I decided it was time to put my travelling days on hold for a while until I had paid off the debt. The next day, I went back to work with a severe headache and wondered if it had all been worth it. Of course, it had been.

CHAPTER 17

I MUST HAVE BEEN
WALKING BACKWARDS

Along with the annual pop festival, the Reading area had a surplus
of special events and galas, many of which a lot of us would
attend. Horse racing at Royal Ascot, boating at Henley Regatta, and
tennis at Wimbledon were but a few. The Knoll Hill steam rally was
a popular choice each year, with beautifully preserved old tractors and
locomotives on display. Our previous visit had been a washout and the
only highlight of the day had been when Stef screeched his van to a
halt after he spotted a street sign named Croft Way. Then, armed with
hacksaws and hammers, we sprang into action and, with the perfect
precision of a highly trained commando unit, promptly removed the
sign. This symbol of oppression was taken home as a trophy of the spoils
of war and proudly displayed on my mantelpiece.

This time around, the weather was perfect. The rally had an
assortment of traditional English distractions on tap, including donkey
rides, a fun fair, Morris dancing, and the ever-popular real ale tent. We
soaked up the genial atmosphere on a beautiful sunny day as we enjoyed
the various activities and laughed at the Morris dancers. In between
hooking rubber ducks, knocking coconuts off stands, and dunking for
apples, we managed to be sociable and try out a few casks of ale. Muff,
Cheryl, Orange Peel, Gus, and I relaxed in the beer tent for the rest of

the day, making sure that none of the ale was wasted. Ultimately, the beer did run out, so we were out of there.

Rather than go home to wash and change and maybe sober up a bit, we continued directly to the Boars Head for a couple of pints. Two was all that we were allowed as the strict totalitarian regime that ran the bar took a stance and prevented us from having any more beer. Seemingly they were under the ridiculous misconception that we'd had too much to drink. After a futile protest, we were slung out on our arses. We dusted ourselves down and concluded that the night was over and that it would be unwise to try and get served in another bar.

So with a feeling of dejection, we moseyed towards Jesse Terrace via Smelly Alley. This popular thoroughfare between Friar Street and Broad Street got its name from the pungent whiff in the air, which emanated from the bustling fish shops in the area. I walked ahead as Neil, Gus, Muff, and Cheryl followed behind, babbling on about this and that. Then out of nowhere, a ferocious shark-toothed demon appeared before my blurred eyes and blocked the alleyway. This phantom was no doubt after my blood, so I took defensive action and aimed a kung fu kick at the mischievous fiend's head.

As I attempted to put the boot into this ghostly illusion, I instead put it through the sizeable front window of a butcher's shop. As if in slow motion, a cracking tentacle extended through the pane of glass before exploding into shards, which flew through the air in all directions. Within an instant, I'd sobered up; before the lethal fragments crashed on to the pavement, I'd done a runner and was halfway up Broad Street.

The next thing I can recall was slowly wakening up in my bed with Eugene shaking me. I could hear Cheryl in the background, blubbering, 'It's all his fault, he did it.'

'What's happening?' I groaned.

Then Eugene said, 'They've all been arrested for smashing a big window. Cheryl says you did it.'

Slowly it all began to come back to me; it hadn't been a dream after all.

'Ah no, the dopey bastards, they were too slow. It's not my fault they got caught,' I said.

'Well, you're going to have to go down to the police station because they're going to charge one of them,' he replied.

'Yes, you have to own up to it. Otherwise, Muff will be in jail all night,' sobbed Cheryl.

'Ballicks to this! I was fast asleep,' I grumbled.

I pulled a T-shirt over my head as I begrudgingly got dressed; then I headed down to the cop shop. Saturday night was usually a hectic time down at the Thames Valley Police HQ, and this night was no exception. The desk sergeant seemed overwhelmed, as he processed drunks and mental cases who were dragged up before him by arresting officers. There were no hookers being escorted in for questioning in the background as on American TV shows, so that was a bit disappointing. It took a while for me to get the sergeant's attention, but when I did, he showed little interest in listening to my confession.

'Let the other three go. I was the one that smashed the big windie,' I pleaded.

With the merest of glances in my direction, he mumbled, 'I've no idea what you're on about. If it has something to do with the broken butcher's window, then you're too late. Someone's already been charged.'

'Well, discharge him. It's me you want. I'm yer man,' I continued.

'Go away. I'm too busy,' he went on, clearly not concerned about what I had to say.

Bloody typical, I thought. *The peelers stop me left, right, and centre for nothing. Now when I'm trying to get lifted, they totally ignore me.* I had to get noticed to save my mates, so I turned up the volume to try to rattle this clown's cage.

I yelled at him, 'Listen. Let the others go. I *smashed the big windie!*'

At last, he raised his eyes to see that I was really there. 'What's your problem? Calm down. Give me your name and address.'

His attitude had now changed as he summoned another officer to take my statement. The new chap wasn't a bad lad and advised me that I'd be kept in overnight and hopefully my friends would be released.

'You've got three good mates down there,' he said. 'None of them were ever going to squeal on you. In fact, your friend Neil has had his boot sent off to forensics and is in the process of being charged,' he explained further.

When the constable had finished my paperwork, he marched me down to the cells and pointed out where the other three were incarcerated.

After my door was bolted, I began shouting out through the peephole, hoping to reach the others, 'I've handed myself in. You can tell them the truth now, and you'll be able to get out!'

Everything was silent; as I hadn't received a response, I was unsure if they knew it was me or not. After calling out a few more times, I assumed that they could not hear me, and I slumped down on to my bed, ready for a long night and not knowing if they'd be set free. A few minutes later, I heard some bizarre noises coming from the other side of my door; they were similar to the sounds that Bluebottle from *The Goons* might make.

Before I was locked up, my shoes had been removed and left in the hallway, but now for some curious reason, they were being stuffed under the door and back into my cell by persons unknown. Curiously, I edged towards the cell door, eager to try to catch a glimpse of the mysterious shoe shuffler. I looked into the peephole, only to see a large wide open bloodshot eyeball staring directly into mine, causing me to jump back from the door. When I regained my composure and took a second look, I realised that it was none other than Muff on the other side, pacing back and forth in the hallway.

I shouted out to him, 'Oy, Muff, what are you doing out there?'

He squeezed his big grinning Duffy Moon face against the peephole and, in a whisper, said, 'They must have forgotten to lock my cell. I leaned against the door and fell out into the hallway, so now I'm just strolling around.'

'Oh aye, it had to be your door, didn't it? Go over and tell the others that I've owned up to it and you should be all be released soon,' I said.

'OK,' he replied and sauntered across the hall to their doors.

It didn't take long before the innocent three were sent back to their loved ones, although Neil had to make the trip home minus one boot; the other was on a holiday to the crime lab in London.

Upon release, I realised that my moment of madness had severe consequences; a charge of criminal damage was looming on the horizon, and if found guilty, I would be in shit street. It would be unlikely that they'd lock me up for such an offence, though it could be a possibility if I was unable to pay off the inevitable fine. On my meagre wages, it would mean that I'd be paying a large chunk to the Crown for the next few years, so I had to start selling my assets immediately. I did an inventory check of my belongings to see how much money I could raise. It didn't take long. One digital alarm clock radio at the going rate of about 2 pounds meant that my total funds available would be . . . 2 pounds. I couldn't even sell my shoes as I'd be limiting my prospective clients to males with one foot bigger than the other. Simon suggested that I seek out the help of a lawyer that he had used in the past; he said that it was possible I could get legal aid to offset any upfront payments. I had to take a chance; perhaps this wise old sage could reduce my pain slightly.

Soon I was promptly off down town to meet with the learned Right Honourable Mr Percy Robinson. The office was opposite the post office in Friar Street, and upon arrival, I took a deep breath and entered.

'I'd like to talk to Mr Robinson, if I may,' I said, attempting to speak in a refined English accent. 'He was highly recommended by one of his previous clients.'

'Oh, I'm sorry, but I'm afraid Mr Robinson has recently decided to retire,' said an older but shaggable secretary.

Just brilliant, I thought, *I haven't even met the old bastard, but he's already let me down.* It was a dilemma. What was my next move? Scratching my head, I did an about turn and walked out of the office. Just before I had closed the door the lady called me back.

'Excuse me, but I can send you through to Mr Jenkins if you wish. He will be taking over any old or new cases on Mr Robinson's files,' she said.

Without much choice, I returned and agreed to meet the intern. He was an odd dishevelled human being; he was unshaven and had a mat of hair scattered about his head as if he'd just arrived on a motorbike. His clothes could easily have been donated from Oxfam. The sports jacket was the typical hippie herringbone twill with leather patches on the elbows. His off-white shirt was partially unbuttoned, with the tail hanging out. First impressions were not good, and when he eventually introduced himself in a series of sporadic pauses due to an intermittent stutter, I was convinced that I was done for.

He offered me one of his sweaty palms. 'Good m-m-morning, Mr Croft, pl-pl-pleased to meet you,' he stammered.

I explained my predicament and asked if he had ever come across something like this before.

'Well, actually, Mr Croft, th-th-this will be my first-ever case,' he said.

Brilliant, I thought. *Just my luck. I've been lumbered with an apprentice lawyer.*

On a plaque outside the building, the advertisement indicated that they were practising law, but I didn't think it would be as literal as that.

'I was hoping that you could help reduce my fine, but if this is your first case, maybe I should go somewhere else,' I said somewhat politely.

'Reduce ya-your fine? I'll d-do better than that. I'll g-g-get you legal aid and g-g-get you off all charges,' he nearly said.

He was confident if nothing else, and that was without even knowing what I'd done. For all he knew, I could have been slicing up people for the last ten years. As I was skint, legal aid was the clincher for me. Get it, and he was my man.

A couple of months had passed when the dreaded letter arrived. I was to appear at the Reading courthouse the following Monday morning. The prosecution was fired up and prepared to do me for deliberately smashing the butcher's window. My rookie lawman, on the other hand, had planned to fight the charge on the grounds that it was accidental and that alcohol was a defining factor. Muff, Gus, and Orange Peel would be called as witnesses. I arrived to be greeted by Mr Ballard (Mr Bollocks), the evil prosecutor. He had made his presence known previously down at the police station and didn't hold back on the fact that he felt that I was guilty and that he hated me. It seemed to be personal to this joker, which made me feel that I would soon be toast.

Upon leaving he ran a finger across his throat in a cutting motion to indicate that I was done for. It was not the first time that I'd been up in front of the Crown, but a negative outcome on this occasion could send me packing back to the troublesome shores of Northern Ireland. In the gallery were a couple of journalists and a few nosy bastard members of the public as well as my trusty musketeers, ready to do battle. The judge was female, so I wasn't sure if she'd fall in love with my Gaelic charm or realise that I was a conniving pig-dog straight from the backstreets of Belfast. So it began.

Immediately my adversary went up 1–0 when a clerk of the court summoned Muff with a loud booming voice, 'Call Mark Smith!'

There was a pause.

'Call Mark Smith!'

Another pause.

'Call Mark Smith!'

After a few murmurs and rumblings from the bench, they concluded that Mark Smith was not amongst the audience. It was not a good start and I wondered how much damage this would do to my battle against the Crown. Gus and Orange Peel laughed out a string of nervous giggles that by no means helped my cause.

Then the clerk continued, 'Call Neil Pettet!'

This time Neil was on his toes and up to the dock like an agitated whippet that had downed a few Dexy's. He was perspiring heavily and twitching like a . . . twitcher. The clerk placed a Bible down and asked Neil to put his right hand on it and say after him: 'I swear by Almighty God that I'll tell the truth, the whole truth, and nothing but the truth.'

But before Neil was finished, the prosecution had taken a 2–0 lead. His brain deactivated upon sight of the Holy Book, and then he turned into a babbling idiot.

'I swear by all rhymey rord that I—sorry, I swear by all rhymey gord—No, wait a minute. I mean, God, all rhyemey God. No, that's not it either.'

His tongue seemed to lose traction, and he just kept spouting nonsense. They decided to skip the Bible bit as the case had to be completed within the allocated time. He then answered every question with a simple yes or no, and it was hard to say if that was a good thing or a bad thing.

Gus was up next. It appeared as if Mr Bollocks had found a discrepancy in his statement, and he quickly went on the attack, using highly confrontational tactics.

He thought he had Gus on the ropes and demanded an explanation. 'Mr Pithouse, in your earlier statement, you said you were in front of Mr Croft when the window was broken, but now you say you were behind him. How can this be?'

Gus hesitated then looked directly at the inquisitor and replied, 'I must have been walking backwards.' His statement seemed to mystify the listeners throughout the courtroom, triggering a ripple of murmured curiosity.

The baffled prosecutor retreated and announced, 'No further questions.'

It was now possibly a 3–0 advantage to the Crown: a surely insurmountable lead. The ever-eager Mr Jenkins rose to my defence in an effort to reduce the deficit. He spoke to the court of past cases when the accused was intoxicated and because of this state of mind, did not deliberately carry out any of the damages. I was surprised by how meticulous my defender was as he shuffled through reams of pages from a remarkably hefty law book. The judge appeared at ease with the contents of his oration, but the prosecution seemed to have an air of satisfaction that the information would not be applicable to my case.

When he had completed his synopsis, I was called to the dock. The obnoxious Mr Bollocks immediately began to attack my character and background, arguing that a Belfast nurturing meant that I was without doubt a bad one. He went on to conclude that it seemed only natural that I should indulge in certain disagreeable activities. My back was to the wall. I was in trouble and had no idea of how to respond to Mr Bollocks's relentless grilling. He questioned me and demanded that I explain my actions on that particular evening.

I sighed nervously and began to speak. 'I was in a good mood walking down Smelly Alley, waving my arms and legs about, when I accidentally slipped and my foot went through the window,' I said.

'Oh, I see, you accidentally slipped. How convenient. You were just strolling along, waving your arms and legs about? Is this the way that a rational person might walk?' he asked.

After pondering momentarily, I countered with the first thing that came to mind: 'There's always risk in movement!'

'What does that mean? What are you talking about?' he croaked and stepped back to his desk. He grappled for a glass of water to clear his throat, then loosened the top button of his shirt, and wiped an anxious finger around the collar.

He mumbled, 'There's always risk in movement? Ahem. No further questions.'

Mr Bollocks seemed rattled. Mr Jenkins advised the bench that he had nothing to add, so the judge rose and announced an adjournment. Gus and Neil joked around, trying to take my mind off the uneasy circumstances during the short interlude, but it seemed evident that the verdict would not go my way.

After a half hour deliberation, the judge strode back into the arena with all the power in the world to send me to the gallows. She looked pensive as she tapped the relevant sheets of paper down on the mahogany countertop, squaring each page symmetrically.

The audience hushed as she read out the ruling, 'Not guilty.'

Before those words were spoken, my heart had been racing like a runaway train, but gradually it skidded back into a steady rhythm after the judge's favourable conclusion. A victory! I'd defeated the Crown's nasty little prosecution team!

My two compatriots rushed to join me in a triumphant jig, and I thanked Mr Jenkins for his fine defensive work. The snivelling Mr Bollocks, on the other hand, went into a mental fit, ranting and raving at the bench about the underhanded wrongdoing. When the judge agreed to my counsel's request for legal aid, he flipped completely. He pleaded to have me bound over for a probationary period even though I had been found not guilty. Mr Bollocks did not stop there; he was all over the place, demanding that at least Gus or Neil should be bound over.

Eventually, he was sent scurrying from the courtroom by the irate judge, who rebuked the out-of-control prosecutor over his tirade and emphasised that neither of them were on trial. Before I left, the judge advised me that the fee to replace the butcher's window was 130 pounds and that as I was to receive 150 pounds in legal aid, the decent thing to do was to cover the costs. I nodded my head in agreement, grabbed the cheque, and was promptly off to the Boars Head, with Gus and Neil struggling as usual to keep up.

We took the long way around, avoiding Smelly Alley. During my celebratory pint, I'd calculated that as the lawyer's fees were 90 pounds and factoring in the legal aid package, I'd made a profit of 60 pounds—a nice little earner indeed. Of course, I sort of promised the judge that I'd pay for the window, but taking into account that the butcher had already used his insurance money to replace it, why should I clog up the system with extra paperwork?

CHAPTER 18

THE ABDUCTION OF
THE LONELY PRINTER

Tom's flooring business was expanding, so he relocated the stores of TW Flooring to bigger premises in Howard Street and rented out the upstairs two-bedroom flat to Simon and Dave. Situated between Jesse Terrace and the town centre, this became an ideal place to stop off, either going to or coming from the newly opened Fives Bar. The Boars Head had started going downhill rapidly, so it was the right time to change pubs, and the Fives was a perfect setting.

Each weekend, after the pub closed, there would usually be a mini party at Howard Street that was finished off at Jesse Terrace. Simon and Dave were both easygoing, and although they didn't always agree that there should be a party, they never protested much when one occurred. They were good mates who could easily have been the stars of the movie *The Odd Couple*: Dave being clean, tidy, and rational; Simon being rarely at home.

Each year, someone would offer up their accommodation as a venue to view the FA Cup final. This time around, it was Simon and Dave's turn, so on a Wednesday evening in 1981, we all piled into the flat for the final; coincidentally, it was also my birthday. It was the replay of a 1–1 draw the previous Saturday; Ricky Villa stole the return game by scoring two memorable goals to help Tottenham Hotspur defeat

Manchester City by 3–2. Then it was over to Fives Bar for a few more tipples and an extended birthday celebration.

The apartment was always well groomed, and I'd help to keep it that way by checking in to inspect their fridge for any out-of-date edible arrangements. They had real food: fresh meats, vegetables, French loaves, and various cheeses. It was a proper flat. The view was nothing to behold though. A building site for the future Ramada Hotel offered an unfortunate vista; meanwhile, the IDR (the main artery through the town to Oxford) did nothing to embellish the backdrop. But who needed scenery when you could enjoy fine foods and beer whilst listening to the new Bruce Springsteen LP, *The River*? Simon had recently acquired it, and to my delight, I found that 'Hungry Heart' was the perfect track to help me tidy up their cheese collection by squaring off any edges to make the blocks nice and symmetrical. Dave was never too happy about this, but it had to be done.

One Saturday morning, Simon was bored and turned up at Jesse Terrace in his Ford Capri, wondering if anyone would like to go somewhere for a drive. Eugene and I were the only ones around, and as we had nothing to do, we let him talk us into joining him on his impulsive adventure. He said that Dave was in housewife mode after returning from his printing job, covered in ink. As he was a bit short on cash, he'd planned to spend the day cleaning the flat after doing his laundry. Dave saved a lot of his earnings in those days and later became very successful running his own business.

We drove past the flat in Howard Street en route to the unknown where we spotted the carefree printer. He was walking towards the Oxford Road, armed with a black plastic bag containing his dirty laundry. Simon suggested kidnapping him, so we cruised up behind the startled hobo, who was dressed in an ink-stained off-white T-shirt and grubby undersized track bottoms. Eugene and I jumped out of the two-door Capri and, with the precision of an SAS snatch squad, bundled Dave into the back seat. He was kicking and squealing like a stuck pig, but Eugene lay on top of him, allowing Simon to accelerate and zoom off through the town towards the M4.

Dave yapped and moaned non-stop, demanding that he be released back into the community, but we ignored his whinging and kept on going. He finally settled down a bit when Simon swerved at high speed on to the motorway. There was no turning back, and Dave knew his fate was sealed as he joined us on the road to nowhere.

'Where are we going?' he asked.

'To London to see the Queen,' replied Simon.

'I'm dressed like a tramp and have no money,' he moaned.

'Don't worry. We'll lend you some cash,' said Simon.

There was not much that Dave could do to change the state of affairs, so he finally calmed down and tolerated the forty-five-minute trip to destinations unknown. Without much thought of where we'd actually go when we got to London, it was suggested that as Wimbledon was in full swing, we should give it a whirl.

The famous old tennis village was packed with tourists who were scurrying from shop to shop in search of an elusive bargain. The traditional tub of strawberries and cream was going for an extortionate fee of five pounds a portion. Not that that concerned the exclusive upper-class twits.

Our first stop was at a beautiful old pub which was adorned with a thatched roof. We promptly established ourselves at a corner table in a cosy alcove, where we could watch the horse racing on the large TV. The inn was busy, with a mixture of regulars and a few smartly dressed part-time tennis junkies. Although we were not exactly fashion models, Simon, Eugene, and I were dressed appropriately for the occasion, but Dave looked as if he was on a day release from a homeless shelter. The bum was also penniless, so we had a whip around to lend him a few shillings each.

Later we kicked back and relaxed with a couple of pints and decided to chance our luck with a little flutter on the ponies. The short eight-furlong sprint meant that the wager was not about to last long as we watched our carthorses slide to the back of the pack, but for golden-balls David, it was a different story. It didn't seem worth it when he backed the odds on favourite Shergar, a bet that would not have even doubled his money. However, unknown to us, he had slyly used the borrowed money to gamble on a straight forecast, and a 66–1 outsider finished second behind Shergar. In an instant, he'd gone from being an impoverished punter on an involuntary excursion to Jack the Lad with around eighty quid in his skyrocket. Before the end of the day, we were borrowing money from him. Although he had lifted the equivalent of a week's wages, he didn't deem it necessary to purchase a new T-shirt to replace the gravy-stained rag he was wearing.

Next it was on to the All England Lawn Tennis and Croquet Club. The plan was to make it to Aorangi Terrace, the hill outside the show courts. However, we first had to pay a two-pound entrance fee, after which we would make our way through a set of turnstiles that led to the outside courts. Some of the lower seed matches were already in progress, and we could just about observe them by squeezing our faces through the metal railings. Was two pounds a reasonable fee to watch a few no-names play? We thought not and commenced to climb up and over the fencing, being vigilant not to be gored by the spiked topper. The outside courts were accessible to anyone who had entered through the turnstiles, and that technically included ourselves even if we had climbed over instead.

Uninterested in the peripheral challengers of the lawn tennis extravaganza, we made our way onward to the elite number-one and centre courts. This area was buzzing with class, with the two main courts securely guarded by members of Her Majesty's forces. Our aim was to sneak in to one of the games already in progress, but it seemed futile. Both venues were filled to capacity as people watched Bjorn Borg take on Vitas Gerulaitis in the centre court and John McEnroe in competition with Stan Smith in court number 1.

Next, we tried our luck at the exclusive Renshaw Cocktail Lounge for the rich and famous, which was obviously not open to street reprobates such as ourselves. The burly security guards made it evident that we were not welcome and ushered us away from the lavish club's foyer. Looking up at the many celebrities with martinis in hand on the scenic glass balconies increased Simon's desire to gatecrash the party. The enormous grunters on the door would surely rip our heads off if we attempted to bypass them in pursuit of a forbidden cocktail. We needed a plan, so Eugene and I duly obliged by staging a quarrel in front of the robust bouncers.

'Oy, big nose, what are you looking at?' I yelled at him.

'Who are you calling big nose? You're one to talk!' he replied and grabbed me around the neck.

We hit the ground, shouting obscenities at each other and forcing onlookers to step back, as they understandably did not want to be involved in the commotion. Rather than letting our little melee escalate and upset some highly influential guests, the security staff on guard at the club's foyer intervened to terminate the scuffle. In the short moment that the front entrance was unprotected, Simon made his move. With the stealth of a Thomson's gazelle, he bounded up the plush stairway into the All England Tennis and Croquet Club.

After a stern reprimand, Eugene and I were told to beat it, and the doormen marched back to their sentry posts, oblivious to the great caper that we'd just pulled off. Dave, Eugene, and I positioned ourselves away from the scene of the disturbance, out of sight of the agitated security guards. We shifted our eyes up to the club's balcony, waiting in hope to see if Simon had cracked the code, and sure enough, he did not let us down.

He sauntered out on to the veranda like Cary Grant, grinning like a Cheshire Cat, and scooped a martini from a vacant table. No sooner had he sipped from the glass when an extended arm emerged from the shadows. An oversized hand clasped around Simon's neck and yanked him off his feet back into the abyss. In one smooth movement, the club's foyer doors opened, the security guards parted, and Simon came hurtling down the stairs and rolled out into the yard like a discarded carpet.

An appreciative cheer broke out from passing observers, not unlike what you might hear following a booming ace delivered from Bjorn Borg's racket. Simon stood up, dusted himself down, and joined us in a well-earned moment of jovial banter.

Mission accomplished. Next stop: centre court.

The All England Club foray was really a one-man assignment, but getting into the top courts would not be a success unless all four of us were to gain the right of entry. The centre court was our main objective, but after we cased the joint for a while, the exercise was abandoned due to a heavy naval presence patrolling the main entrance gates. Number 1 court seemed feasible, though. We studied the actions of a Royal Air Force unit during interludes and noticed a pattern evolving: occasionally, some of them would leave their post for refreshments.

A generous round of applause went up at the end of the first set, creating a buzz of activity; then a few spectators decided to stretch their legs. A small percentage of them chose to hover by the entrances. It was then that we sprang into action, mingling with the crowd before ducking past the hapless armed forces and down into the depths of the arena. Four spare seats were available together a few rows back from the pristine grass court. Casually, we sidled into position and waited patiently to be kicked out.

'New balls please!' was the umpire's cry as the stands began to fill up, and McEnroe and Smith limbered up, preparing to start a new set.

Directly in front of us, an older American couple and a spotty-faced teenager sat down to block the excellent view that we had had before. The woman was whining loudly about the English weather, and the old fellow blocked my view when he pulled a wide-brimmed hat over his balding head.

'I'm gonna pull his hat off and fling it on to the court,' I said.

'You'll get us flung out. Leave the old fellow alone. Say nothing,' replied Dave. He was right; I'd forgotten that we didn't have tickets and so far, we had been lucky as no one had yet claimed the seats that we had appropriated. We later found out that the old farts were John McEnroe's parents and that the spotty kid was his brother, Patrick, who would also go on to be a professional tennis player.

Surprisingly, no one ever did come back to retrieve their expensive seats, and we saw out the remainder of the match, watching McEnroe defeat Smith in straight sets. At the end of the day, just as the last ace was struck, Dave had long forgotten how his unforeseen abduction had played out. By the time the chalk dust had settled, he had scooped up not only a tasty payday at the bookies but also a ringside seat where he saw the future Wimbledon champ in action—thanks to the generosity of the All England Tennis and Croquet Club.

It wouldn't be long before those out-of-the-blue car rides into the unknown would end. Simon had gotten well in with Steve, the owner of Fives Bar, by helping him run the place if he was unable to make it into Reading on some occasions. Steve trusted him so much that when he opened another Fives Bar in Bedford, Simon was offered the opportunity to relocate and become the manager. Although we missed him and did visit from time to time, the move worked out to perfection for Simon.

It wouldn't be long before he was back to Reading to run the Fives Bar there. It was brilliant: our favourite watering hole was now in the hands of one of our best mates. He revamped the place by adding televisions that constantly played the top music videos, and the name was changed to the New Yorker. People would hover outside, watching 'Thriller' and other classic videos before being enticed in for a drink. The doors shut at 11 p.m., but for us, there was no closing time.

CHAPTER 19

A DEAD POLISH WOMAN IN BAKER STREET

We were to lose a few stars in 1981. They included actor William Holden, musicians Bill Haley and Bob Marley, and ex-heavyweight champ Joe Louis, 'the Brown Bomber'. And who did we get to replace these recently deceased leading lights? It was the birth year of Beyoncé Knowles, Britney Spears, Justin Timberlake, and the incomparable Paris Hilton. Enough said.

Other notable events of that year included *Postman Pat* airing for the first time on BBC 1 and Muhammad Ali losing to Trevor Berbick, thus bringing the curtain down on his career. Also, the Egyptian president Anwar Sadat was assassinated by army members belonging to the Islamic Jihad organisation because he had a chat with Israel, and Mauritania abolished slavery. 'Don't You Want Me' was asked by the Human League, Duran Duran gave us 'Girls On Film', and Men at Work explained that they were in fact from 'Down Under'. But as with every great song, there was a conglomeration of shit to follow. We were not surprised when Joe Dolce was told to 'Shaddap You Face', the Tweets drove everyone nuts with 'The Birdie Song', and Cliff Richard's 'Daddy's Home' made us throw up for the longest time.

Michael had returned from Saudi Arabia with his head and ball bag still intact. The UK government had reminded him that there were some unresolved monetary irregularities that needed his attention, so he'd planned to remain in Reading for a few months before heading back to play in the desert. He'd found a nice little top-floor flat in Baker Street just around the corner from Jesse Terrace. To the consternation of the rest of the motoring community, he'd picked up an old Ford Cortina and was back on the road again. The high court thought they had made the streets of Reading safe again by confiscating his Northern Ireland driving licence and imposing a lengthy ban.

What legal authorities did not take into consideration was that there was a possibility that he might have held an English licence as well. And of course, he did. Michael also had two passports: one in his own name and the other under the pseudonym Peter Johnston. This was a little knick-knack that he'd picked up in Amsterdam in exchange for some dodgy pieces of Saudi gold. Things were never dull when Michael was around. He was a terrible driver and the only person I knew who was more likely to kill someone when he was sober than when he was drunk.

There was a big party that we were not really invited to out near Wokingham, so naturally we would attend the event. Michael volunteered to be the designated driver, but he had previously had a few drinks, so we felt somewhat safe. Eugene, Neil, and Gus were also in the car, and we knew vaguely where the house was. As we approached the locale, it was quite obvious that the large lit-up house blasting out the sounds of *the Clash* was the one we were looking for. Michael was in one of his unbalanced moods and knowingly passed by without stopping. When we pointed out that he had missed the house, he jammed on the anchors, did a quick about-turn, and sped back in the direction of the party. But once again he kept on motoring past our destination. Michael made the same manoeuvre two more times without acknowledging that he'd even seen the house. He was definitely playing dopey bollocks, and we were getting pissed off. I waved my hand across his face to try to get a response, but his brain was now being controlled by aliens.

'If you don't stop at the house next time, you'll be getting a slap!' I yelled into his lughole.

It didn't make any difference; he kept on driving, eyes fixed ahead with an inert stare, as if it were Groundhog Day. We again slowed down outside the party; then as he began to speed up, I opened my door in a potentially fatal move.

'You're a nutter. I'm getting out!' I exclaimed in frustration.

Then I lunged from the car. I'd planned to roll myself out and away on to the grass verge and then bound up like Spider-Man, ready for business. Unfortunately, my action-hero exploits were thwarted when I crunched against a higher-than-normal kerb, ending up face down in the gutter. Michael skidded to a halt, but before I could crawl away from the side of the road, he'd slammed the car into reverse. In my peripheral vision, I could see the tail lights of the Cortina hurtling towards me as I lay helplessly, awaiting my demise. I'd like to think that Michael spotted my powerless body and took evasive action to avoid squashing me flat. It was probably not the case though, and my life was likely saved because he was such a bad driver that he was unable to keep any car moving in a straight line.

Although he'd swerved enough to sidestep a direct hit, the passenger door was still open, and it skewered the cheeks of my arse and picked me up like a human doner kebab. Michael finally landed back on the same planet and only brought the car to a halt after hearing me squealing out like a pig on the way to the slaughterhouse. The backside of my jeans had been torn away, exposing an elongated wound that leaked abundantly on to the white car door, creating an artistic raspberry ripple effect. I was helped to my feet by the others, limped over to the party, and went straight into the bathroom to wash and dress my battle scar. Michael disappeared soon after that.

My partying was limited to sitting in the corner of the main room on an iced cushion to stem the flow of claret from my bum cheek. It was just my luck that the place was teeming with tasty women on the lookout for a shag. Some of them were curious about my injury, but any slim chance that I could pull one of them went out the window when they found out that I was in fact a person with two bum holes. The evening was a write-off as I became a literal pain in the bottom and opted for a lift back to the Battle Hospital emergency unit for some much-needed treatment. That night just happened to be the changing of the guard as far as emergency departments were concerned at Reading area hospitals. The Battle trauma unit ceased to be as of midnight and closed its doors. Everything shifted to the Royal Berkshire Hospital, but this extreme move took time, so anyone who had been carved up between the hours of 12 a.m. to 7 a.m. that morning was shit out of luck. It was not a great time to get one's arse sliced open, so I had to stem the bleeding for another six hours. Eventually, I was sewed up and entertained a few nurses in the process.

Michael signed a contract for another year in Saudi Arabia and asked if I would be interested in residing in his penthouse apartment in Baker Street while he was away. The last couple of years living in Jesse Terrace had been a blast, but it was perfect timing for me to make the move. It would be a lot more private, and I'd have a key to keep people out, unlike the revolving French windows to my room, which were currently used by most passers-by. Another bonus would be the luxury of waking to my own alarm as opposed to being shaken from my slumber by the unceremonious buzzing of Eugene's clock. I wouldn't particularly miss the daily routine of rising one hour prematurely to whisper softly into his shell-like to inform him in a gentlemanly tone that he should prepare himself for work.

Although he had originally planned to stay for only a few weeks, the tenancy had by now lasted for close to a year. Eugene would now be the sole lodger in the master bedroom and would at last have a real bed to sleep in as opposed to a mattress on the floor. However, with that came the added challenge of keeping up with the allotted household chores, some of which he ultimately failed to carry out. He would later be chastised by Hazel for not putting the bins out enough.

The adventures of Michael were a bittersweet affair. Although he was a great friend of mine, the chances that I would end up wrapped round a lamppost or in jail greatly increased while he was around. Then again, I had often feared for him when he was in Saudi Arabia, getting up to God knows what. Ultimately, he once again took the subversive path that the oil industry offered and headed back to the Sahara Desert, leaving me to pack up my rubber duck and digital alarm clock radio and make the 200-yard move to his Baker Street flat.

Life didn't change much as I assumed my independence. Most of the time, I'd be hanging out at Jesse Terrace and only used my bachelor pad to sleep in. Michael had warned me about the landlord being a miserable, tight old bastard who didn't give much away. He and his wife were Polish, spoke very little English, and lived on the main floor and basement levels of the large house. Michael's electric bill was included in his rent payments, but there was a limit on how much he could use as he found out in a bizarre way.

On those rare early-to-bed occasions, he was partial to snuggling up with an obscure book, looking for inspirational pieces to add to his routine mischief portfolio. One such evening, around midnight, he heard the bedroom door creak open slightly. Out of the corner of his eye, he saw a wrinkly old hand snake along the wall to flick the light switch off and then retract back into the darkness. The phantom of late-night energy saving then grumbled in broken English as he tiptoed away from the room, 'No use electric. Too late.'

Cold baths were normal from Monday to Friday as the hot water heater was only turned on at the weekend. Michael had had his fair share of bust-ups with the old git, but the landlord would wave his hands in the air and turn a deaf ear, claiming a limited understanding of the English language. I had to adapt to the draconian rules and regulations of my Polish landlord. The 'no baths until Saturday' law was beneficial to my fitness levels as I would go straight from work to the swimming pool for a dip and scrub-down. Alas, this was to last less than one week. The staff barred me from entering the facility until I'd cleaned my act up. At that time, I had shoulder-length high hair that resembled the bearskin hats worn by Her Majesty's guards outside Buckingham Palace. At the end of a day, after some hard graft on the building sites, my busby would be caked in concrete dust and other miscellaneous materials. Upon entering the changing rooms, I'd sling my dusty work clothes into a locker and then sprint to the poolside clad in my electric blue Speedos. Then like Mark Spitz, I'd soar like a salmon and plonk into the refreshing crystal clear water, leaving a mushroom cloud of construction dust rising towards the ceiling. Any other patrons out for a leisurely dip witnessed an assortment of nasty particles settle back into the pool like the aftermath of a nuclear fallout. So I had to resign myself to bathing at the weekends and boiling a kettle to wash my bits in the kitchen sink throughout the week.

During my time at Jesse Terrace, I had been given some leeway as far as paying the rent on time each week was concerned. Tom would usually let it pass for a while and then threaten to tear my head off if the piss was taken. My new landlord was uncharted territory. I would go down to the kitchen each week with ten quid, and the wife would slip it into a brown envelope without ever saying a dickie bird. Whether she was uncomfortable with her limited use of the English language or just shy, I did not know.

One month, I had pushed my luck a bit by missing two weeks' rent, but as no one had asked me for the cash, I thought I'd ride it out to see how long I could get away with it. Later I began to worry that they might kick me out without warning, so I eased my way down the stairs with twenty pounds, hoping they'd forget how much was owed. The night before, a police car and ambulance had been parked outside the house, and that had got my mind working overtime. I tapped softly on the kitchen door, expecting the little old lady to appear, but instead the miserable old bastard stomped from the room in a very agitated state.

Uh-oh, I thought. Now I'm in for it.

He was anxious and kept repeating: 'You say sorry for my wife. You say sorry.'

'I will. I'm sorry for being late with the rent,' I replied apologetically.

He was hard to understand at the best of times, but this time around, he was excelling and making a right bollocks of his pigeon English.

He continued his rant. 'No, no, you say sorry for my wife. She gone, she gone.'

By now I was thinking that the shy petite woman had finally had enough of the cantankerous old fool and up and left him.

I tried to soften the blow. 'I will say sorry when I see her next time.'

Then he broke down and wept: 'No, no, she gone. She *dead*!'

Stunned, I stepped back and shook my head. He'd been trying to tell me that she was gone, gone for good; she was taidy bread! The police, the ambulance—it began to fall into place. She'd died while I'd been watching *The Dukes of Hazzard*. The old fella was in a terrible state, so I retreated deftly into the hallway as his salty tears streamed down his craggy boat race. Not wanting to burden this grief-stricken soul with the trivial monetary issues of amounts outstanding, I stuffed the rent money back into my pocket and headed for the hills. Alas, as they say, one man's misfortune is another man's gain. He'd lost his wife, but I was up thirty quid.

The times, they were a-changing. The snowball effect was taking place as one by one we relinquished our status of being single. Things happen for whatever reason, and for me, hooking up with Nancy again seemed inevitable, although the bookies would still have given us odds of 100–1 that we'd stay together for more than two years. Our paths had crossed in an unusual way on a flight of stairs at a get-together in Oxford. She had slipped on the top landing and then began a foot-first descent, bouncing her arse against each tread during the rough ride. The tricky manoeuvre ended with a sudden crash at the bottom, leaving her exposed and in a crumpled heap, wedged upside down against a wall. It was a sure way to break the ice at parties.

I had witnessed the whole thing, and like the gentleman I was, I checked on her to make sure no permanent damage had been done. That evening, we arranged to meet secretly the next week for a drink at the Moderation Pub. It seemed to us that the less people that knew about our clandestine encounter, the better. I suggested that she should soon visit me at my penthouse suite in Baker Street, but I pointed out that my landlord would not be happy if she turned up uninvited. There was no doorbell to my flat, so I planned to leave a key in the front door latch, but the timing had to be perfect in order for her to let herself in unnoticed. About ten minutes before she had planned to arrive, I inserted the key in the latch and boiled the kettle for a romantic spot of tea. The scene was set as I relaxed on the sofa with the cups at the ready and a packet of very expensive chocolate Hobnobs scattered suggestively. Then I heard the front door close and the pitter-patter of feet on the staircase. I'd synchronised my digital alarm clock radio and tuned it to an easy listening station. The mood was set as the living room door opened, and I rose to greet . . . Louise?

Instantly she started talking. 'What a day I've had. My boss was moaning at me and—'

'Slow the boat down. What are you doing here?' I spluttered in panic.

Before she could park her arse down, I tried to shove her back out the door, but she gave me a body swerve and plonked herself down. Louise was a girl that I knew who didn't hang around in our circle. Ever since I'd obtained independent living, she stopped by from time to time with bits of chicken and various vegetables and proceeded to wear out my lug. I was sure it was a matter of time before I would shag her, but she had no interest in performing any sexual acts with me. So after a few attempts to get her into bed, I gave up. She was so boring, but she did bring much-needed sustenance, so I let her pop round when I was hungry. But this was a disaster. She'd taken advantage of an invitational key in the door and waltzed on in. Without being rude or dragging her down the stairs by the throat, I somehow got shot of her and was back on the sofa in full pose with seconds to spare. When Nancy arrived, the night went off well, and after a month or so of sneaking about, we announced to the world that we were seeing each other.

Nancy's brother Stuart and his girlfriend, Helen, offered her a nice little flat in Eldon Square, an area inhabited mostly by sophisticated conservatives. It made sense for us to spend more time there as it was a real flat complete with its own front door, kitchen, living room, bedroom, and bathroom. The bonus of full-time hot water at the ready was a major step up from using the kitchen sink as a toilet or somewhere to wash your feet. It was a tastefully furnished little flat, and thanks to the generosity of Woolworth PLC, we eventually acquired a brand-new state-of-the-art stereo record player.

Originally, Nancy had picked up the system that she desired after putting down a ten-pound deposit and negotiating an acceptable weekly payment to cover the full amount. A few days after we had enjoyed listening to our favourite LPs on the turntable, she received a letter from Woolworths indicating that her family had been blacklisted from purchasing anything from the store. They apologised for the inconvenience, citing prior financial irregularities from her relatives. It meant that she would not be able to purchase the stereo system as she was not eligible for credit. The dopey bastards then sent back her ten-pound deposit, oblivious to the fact that she had already taken the stereo system home.

It wouldn't be long before almost everyone in our group had a steady girlfriend, and gradually they began to cohabit. Dave couldn't believe his luck when Jacqui agreed to be his partner. They got on like a house on fire except when it came to sorting out who had the biggest piece of cheese and toast. Eugene began seeing Julie, a girl that he had previously met who had now returned from a kibbutz in Israel. Up until then, we had often enjoyed a few pre-pints and a quiet game of pool in the Comrades Club before moving on to Fives Bar. Julie changed all that by constantly playing the Bucks Fizz shite 'Making Your Mind Up' on the jukebox, thus driving us out of there earlier than we had stayed before. Stef was seeing Lucinda (aka Binders), Muff had met Melinda, Simon went upmarket with a girl called Alison, and Gus started seeing Neil's sister, Debbie. Consequently, instead of running around like single eejits, we ran around like eejits with girlfriends.

CHAPTER 20

A DOG CALLED BOLLOX

At the start of 1982 the unemployment level in the UK had reached 3 million, and the only news worth talking about was that Margaret Thatcher's dim-witted son, Mark, had got lost in the Sahara Desert. I think he mistakenly turned left at Marseilles instead of going straight on during the Paris–Dakar rally. But by April, the country was ready for war after Argentina invaded the Falklands. The headlines each day were about these frosty islands in the South Atlantic that no one had heard of up until then. Names such as Port Stanley and Goose Green were on everyone's tongue, as well as the destruction that the Exocet missile could cause. After an unsure start to the war, all of Britain's spirits were raised by *The Sun* newspaper's headline of 'GOTCHA' after the Argentine cruiser the General Belgrano was torpedoed by the nuclear-powered submarine HMS *Conqueror*. The loss of over three hundred lives—mainly young sea cadets—seemed but a trivial affair.

Top chart hits early in that year had Haircut One Hundred's wanting everyone to have a 'Fantastic Day'; the Stranglers sang 'Golden Brown', which could have been a sexual perversion; and 'The Lion Sleeps Tonight' was cold comfort for Tight Fit because they got their lungs ripped out the next morning when it woke up. I'm sure Bucks Fizz might have released some old shite around then. Tottenham reclaimed the FA Cup by defeating QPR 1–0 in a boring replay after a boring 1–1 draw the first time round, with Glen Hoddle scoring in both games. In

July, a fellow called Michael Fagan woke the queen up after sitting on the end of her bed in Buckingham Palace to see if she'd like some tea. A couple of days later, Italy beat West Germany 3–1 in Spain to win their third World Cup. The greatest game of that tournament was without doubt Northern Ireland's victory over the hosts in Valencia. Gerry Armstrong netted the only goal in the second half to win the group for his country despite Mal Donaghy being sent off for sticking the nut on some Spaniard. The year ended with a victory parade in London for the war in the Falklands, and thousands of women formed a human chain around the perimeter fence of Greenham Common. They forgot to go to work that year.

Before our recently procured girlfriends got the upper hand and began telling us what to do, we had one more trip to Belgium organised. Joyce, a Flemish friend whom Michael had brought to Reading a couple of times, had kindly offered up her apartment in Antwerp to anyone that cared to visit. Six of us were obliged to accept her hospitable proposal. Simon, Dave, Greg, Eugene, Gerry, and I flew from London to Antwerp. We were greeted at the airport by Joyce, who had six cold beers on hand. A fine way to start our escapade indeed! Following a little sightseeing drive through the city, Joyce helped us unload our stuff at the apartment and then handed over the keys. The neat two-bedroom flat was stocked with some fine local provisions, and the fridge was filled with beer. Magic!

The first day we hit the bar and played some pool before kicking back with a few ales at the apartment. Joyce had arranged for us all go to her parents' house for an afternoon lunch and warned us to be on our best behaviour as they were both quite religious. Most of Joyce's friends, including her parents, spoke perfect English, so we had to be aware and mind our language. A couple of cars were dispatched to pick us up and take us to her parents' house. They were lovely people and laid out a veritable spread, including a delightful salad with some of the area's finest cheeses and hams. A beautiful little girl, Els, also resided at the home, and to our surprise, we found out that she was actually Joyce's daughter being raised by her parents. After the feast, we sat about, sipping coffee, responding to her father's inquisitive probing into each of our backgrounds, all the while holding back on the curse words. For most of the afternoon, we played it safe and tended to speak only when spoken to.

Then the arrival of a scraggly old mutt broke the tension. Els ran into the living room, chasing the fiendish canine, which made a beeline for Gerry and began to shag his leg.

She called to the dog, 'Bollox! Get down, Bollox!'

The old hound cowered and slinked into the kitchen with its tail between its legs. This was a chance that we could not let pass.

At last we could officially let off some steam, and in unison, we began to call out: 'Bollocks! Bollocks! Bollocks! Bollocks! Bollocks!'

The poor doggy did not know where to turn as he twisted right and left, trying to respond to the sound of his name. God knows what the translation of the Flemish *bollox* is.

The next day, the chauffeurs arrived to whisk us away to rural Antwerp, where we would immerse ourselves in a bizarre country and Western shindig, the largest in Belgium. We negotiated a small rough road and were eventually greeted by a Flemish John Wayne collecting the entrance fees. After that we made our way into a generous-sized ranch spread across a couple of acres. A rodeo show was in full swing, and bull rides drew gasps of delight as the crazy jockeys were flung into the air. After a sniff around the various enclosures, where we inhaled the fumes of horse and cow shite, we were naturally drawn toward the main pavilion and the Texas-style bar. There we imbibed in some of the world's finest pints of Stella Artois. It was Antwerp's version of the Whitehorse Saloon, filled with drunken cow-people who were singing and line dancing to the sounds of Glen Campbell. It was like watching a good old American Western in double Dutch. Most of the ranch hands were packing heat, but Joyce assured us that six guns' bullets were not live.

As we tried to squeeze our way to the bar, Gerry's progression was halted. He was the kind of person who would do the unexpected and then think about it afterwards. A big dude had blocked his path, and with the use of one finger, Gerry tilted the guy's Stetson back from his forehead, stared into his eyes, and said, 'Hey, man, you look like Jesse James.'

He then withdrew the cowboy's firearm from his holster and brandished the silver revolver in the air. Before he could say 'Remember the Alamo!', the disgruntled Belgian gunfighter clocked Gerry on the chin and laid him out. The compact crowd prevented the Derry man from hitting the deck as he slumped against us. He shook his head a bit, groaned, then asked for a beer, apparently unaware that he'd just been the recipient of a knuckle sandwich.

The place was heaving, and the beer was flowing. We eventually secured a table and settled in to soak up the festive ambience as the crowd sang along with the resident band in the sizeable venue. Although we were a distance away from the stage, the acoustics and the sound system kept everyone in synch and rocking along. Later an interlude saw the band members hit the bar to take a deserved break from the stage. On their way off, they handed the lead over to a strange man in a frilly outfit who addressed the excited crowd.

A lot of activity was taking place amongst the audience, with people frantically writing on handout sheets then rushing them up to the man with the microphone. As his announcement was delivered in Flemish, we had no idea what was occurring. We turned to Joyce for a translation. Apparently, the next hour was a bit of a talent show and a free-for-all for anyone who fancied themselves as an entertainment act. I turned to Eugene and asked him if he was game for a laugh. If so, we could stick our names down on one of the request sheets. All he had to do was play the guitar, and I would sing. With a bit of coaxing from the others, we agreed to give it a go and submitted our ballot. A few acts later, Eugene and I were summoned to the stage, where we received a rapturous reception from the highly intoxicated and fervent crowd.

Then the master of ceremonies announced, this time in English, 'Ladies and gentlemen, it's my pleasure to say welcome to the Belfasters!'

When asked for a stage name, we had panicked and came up with Belfast's equivalent of the Dubliners. The long walk to the front left us a bit anxious as we passed the European cowboys and girls banging their tables, which created a very turbulent atmosphere. A guitar was handed to Eugene as we stepped into the spotlight. There was little time for a rehearsal, so during our walk of fame, Eugene suggested we do 'Rocky Raccoon'. As the crowd settled, he began to strum the intro. I think it might have been stage fright or something, but everything was a clouded haze in front of my eyes, and I blanked on Eugene's opening chords. He played the intro again, expecting me to start crooning, 'Away down in the hills of South Dakota lived . . .', but again, I just stood still with the mic in hand. Eugene was getting pissed off by now, and as he strummed a third introduction, he gave me a look that would have taken a buffalo down and yelled, 'For Christ's sake, *sing*!'

With that, I awoke from my trance. I saw the rabid crowd becoming slightly incensed, possibly mumbling their disapprovals of our act. This time I opened up to belt out McCartney's opening line but then went silent and began to mime the next few words. Eugene was baffled as I continued to sing some parts out loud then silently mumbled the other words. I began to bang the mic as if there were some technical difficulties, thinking this would get the audience rolling in the aisles, taken by my comedic genius. Alas, Eugene wasn't laughing, and neither was the crowd. In fact, it was a massive backfire on my part as it created an air of disdain amongst a now-irate Wild West mob. Instead of basking in the praises of an ecstatic ensemble and getting showered with bouquets of lace panties, we were bombarded with beer slops and soggy napkins. Boos rang out from all around, and we hurriedly made ourselves scarce. The sorry sound of a couple of handclaps echoed from the back of the hall. Dave and Simon were showing their appreciation and support for the Belfasters, but Greg and Gerry lay low, with their heads hidden conspicuously below the table. They just didn't understand what good music was.

Our last evening was a touch more subdued as we enjoyed a stroll amongst the many quaint taverns and cafes in Antwerp's celebrated harbour district. Joyce insisted that we stop for a drink in an unusual bar that had an obvious attraction to the many tourists loitering around its entranceway. She did not indicate exactly what made this particular bar a hotspot for curious sightseers, but we soon found out. Upon entry, we were immediately taken by a pipe-smoking, bearded man sitting alone at a table, nursing a pint of lager. Under normal circumstances, this burly patron would have gone unnoticed, but his attire certainly caught our eye. His heavily tattooed arms were complimented by a beautiful off-the-shoulder light-blue dress with a plunging neckline, exposing a cleavage of copious chest hair. Dotted throughout the bar were an assortment of nautical seadogs conversing with fully grown men who were wearing skirts and completely unfazed by the gazes of the inquisitive visitors.

Joyce expressed her amusement as she observed our varied reactions upon realising that we had stepped into a transvestite bar. Getting a drink in the sideshow would not be easy as the place was heaving, making it almost impossible to get served. When Greg and I finally made it through to order a round, we were taken aback by two stunning blondes serving up the frothy suds. The main bar wench, a big fat bloke in a black dress, wearing a ridiculous wig, stood between the two beauties and strutted his stuff. Joyce joined us at the bar, well aware that we were ogling the gorgeous maidens, and she promptly informed us to back off as they were both fellas. It just did not seem possible; they were probably two of the best-looking girls that I had ever seen.

Greg was as visibly shocked as I was and said to me, 'Could you imagine taking one of them home then slipping a hand between their legs, only to grab a handful of bollocks?'

Looking over his shoulder from behind the bar, the big fat bloke in the black dress and cheap wig chirped back in perfect English, 'They're all the same from the back, honey!' And he continued drying glasses.

We finished the evening off frolicking on a self-styled dance floor with some good arse-skelping music after discovering a record called 'Paddy on the Railway' on the jukebox—just the kind of song one would expect to find in a Flemish transvestite bar. Joyce's parents invited us to the house again for a final meal before we headed off home the next day. Once again, we tucked into an excellent spread laid out by these truly wonderful people. They made sure we knew what Flemish hospitality was and insisted that they should drive us to the airport, where we relaxed with a couple of beers on the short flight back to London. Simon stayed for a while longer to immerse himself in the

Flemish culture—and in a friend that Joyce had introduced to him. A lot was to be learned from this trip. We had discovered that Belgium was a country consisting of two separate peoples living to some extent in relative harmony. There was some discord between the two cultures though, and if it came down to it, I'm sure if there was to be a big scrap, then the Flemish transvestites would surely knock their Walloon counterparts' bollocks in.

CHAPTER 21

THE YUGOSLAVIAN PIE FIGHT

The next planned holiday in Europe was to be with our significant others rather than running wild with the boys. There were some really appealing all-inclusive trips to the old Yugoslavia, and it seemed that four couples were interested. Later, Simon and Alison shit out, as did Muff and Melinda. That left Dave and Jacqui and Nancy and me. We would be flying to Zadar, which is now in Croatia. In fact, it always was; it just didn't know it. I was advised by the other seasoned travellers that it would be hot and that I should wear heavy sunscreen to protect my tender skin. Much like the Scottish, the people of Northern Ireland react dramatically to a bit of sunshine and most of them will say:

'Ack, don't worry, I don't burn.'

But they do burn, very well in fact with an initial light smouldering before full combustion. These northern people start off a shade of pale blue before reaching the white stage, which is a pre-emptive warning that they are about to go up in smoke. During the first few days of our trip, I, of course, took no notice and got instant heat stroke and was forced to spend the first two days hiding in the shade, vomiting violently. The rest of the holiday was a relaxing change though, as we lived life in the slow lane as opposed to getting as many drinks down our necks in the shortest time possible. Maybe the female influence kept it steady; then again, maybe not.

One evening, Dave and I had to make ourselves scarce and get away from the girls, who went on a mental spree. I knew Nancy could be a balloon, but I did not expect Jacqui—the caring, friendly nurse—to blow a gasket. Both of them were blootered and in a dangerous condition. Some irate Germans, one of them waving a tennis racket from the balcony above, began yelling at the girls to be quiet as their children were trying to sleep.

Jacqui's slurred response was 'Who won the war? Shut your mouth and go back to Germany. It's only one thirty in the morning. And why have you got a fishing net in your hand?'

The Germans, of course, kept their distance, as they were petrified of the crazy blonde. That was when Dave and I did a runner, fearing for our lives. We spent the rest of the night in the shadows, sneaking to different bars to avoid our loved ones, who had gone off the rails. We were like commandos, lurking behind darkened walls and then darting into open spaces. The girls made it easy for us to keep our distance as we could hear their big traps from miles away.

A nice calm cruise was up next, and it was just the ticket. The girls were suffering from a mega hangover and hardly opened their mouths for the first hour. I was ready for the occasion, dressed like any sea salt would be in a blue-and-white hooped T-shirt, white shorts, white socks, and white shoes. I looked great. Shortly after the boat sailed from the dock, three musicians playing balalaikas came strutting across the entertainment deck. It sounded reasonable but not quite what was ordered for a hangover. At times, some of the other punters on board would inspect my attire, making me feel like I was some kind of cheap celebrity. It was definitely strange; then I noticed that the three strumming artistes were dressed exactly the same as me. The rest of the passengers obviously thought I was part of the act, so I did a wee Irish jig to let them know I wasn't.

Up next was a cream pie-eating contest with a bottle of champagne for the winner, so Dave and I were in like Flynn. The snag was that each competitor had to be blindfolded, but it didn't cost anything, so why not? Six other people were battling it out for the grand prize, with Dave sitting on my right side and a dodgy-looking Italian geezer on my left. They presented the pies, which were really nothing more than big lumps of whipped cream; then they tied the blindfolds before blowing a whistle. *Splat!* I smacked my face into the gooey mixture and began chomping on down at a rate of knots that seemed impossible for anyone else to match. Then the whistle blew again to the cry of 'We have a winner!'

I removed my blindfold and belched out an enormous burp of satisfaction, convinced that the prize was mine. My air of superiority vanished when I glanced down to see an unspoiled wobbling cream blancmange in front of my eyes. Something was amiss all right. I was covered in cream, but my pie remained intact. Dave's plate was licked clean and he flaunted a mischievous grin as he wiped an arm across his mug to remove any lasting remnants. With that, I picked up my pie and slapped it right into his mush.

'You sneaky bastard, you swapped plates,' I said.

Taken aback by my actions, he clawed the excess particles from his eyes, then grabbed another full soufflé, and pounded it into my face. That was it. War had broken out. We reached for whatever was left of the whipped delights and began battering each other, sending creamy stuff squirting out in all directions. This provided the other appreciative passengers with an unexpected free slice of madcap entertainment. When the commotion finally subsided, Dave revealed that it was not he who had done the dexterous exchange but that it had in fact been the dodgy-looking Italian geezer who sat on my other side. It was a fine piece of legerdemain indeed.

Later that evening, we were joined by the cunning Roman and his wife, who informed us that they in fact lived in England and owned a couple of hotels in London. They seemed like a nice couple and invited us to visit them upon our return to England. He hinted that if we so desired, we could spend the night with them, and he welcomed us to partake in a bit of wife swapping with the Italian stallion. In reality, he was more like a hairy carthorse, and his wife was an old nag ready for the knacker's yard. Dave said that he might be interested but wanted a car thrown in to make it a fair swap.

The next month, Dave, Jacqui, Nancy, and I did visit London, though not to indulge in any form of sexual perversions but to have a meal before taking in a Gary U.S. Bonds concert at the Venue in Victoria. The repast at a Middle Eastern restaurant was unusual to say the least, with Dave taking the chicken bones away for analysis, convinced that he'd been served up rat. Later he found out that all the angst was for naught, as the lab results proved that he certainly did not feast on one of Roland's cousins. The concert was average, with an uneasy feeling of aggro in the air. We were unable to get to our seats and ended up standing in the aisle, dodging flying glasses and bottles thrown by some disruptive reprobates within the crowd. One of the wayward glasses smashed just behind us and cut Nancy on the back of her leg. It was the first time that any of us had been to the Venue, and we decided that it would also be our last.

Later, as we waited outside the main doors for a cab to take us to Paddington, an extremely drunken man began shooting his mouth off at a rather large taxi driver. We assumed that the two had been involved in a previous confrontation as they certainly didn't like each other. The volley of abuse continued back and forth like a tennis rally, but when the drunk flung his can of lager at the taxi, the driver lost it and moved in for an attack. Not wishing to get involved, we stepped back from the fray and distanced ourselves from the inebriated buffoon, who was virtually leaning against us. The aggressive taxi driver delivered one swift blow into the drunk's abdomen, sending him reeling to the floor as he blew out a guttural gasp of air. The driver scampered back to his cab and was off in a flash.

Jacqui, acting instinctively from her training as a nurse, went over to help the downed man to his feet. As she turned him over, some of his internal parts spilled out of a large gash that had separated his belly. The driver had inflicted a deep slice on his foe. Jacqui held his wound closed as best she could as we rushed into the Venue to summon help and call an ambulance. The victim was eased into a back room for further treatment, and Jacqui did her thing. Finally, he was whisked away to the hospital to receive a life-saving surgery. Had it not been for Jacqui's actions that night though, he would have possibly died at our feet.

CHAPTER 22

A FISHY CAPER ON KINGS ROAD

Tom had decided to expand his horizons and agreed to take on a lease at a building near the busy intersection at Jackson's Corner. There he would open up a restaurant and entice the hard-grafting working-class patron to partake in some of the area's finest homemade soups, sandwiches, and burgers. He would also be the first ginger in the land to serve fresh doner kebabs from a typical English-type cafe. With this extravagant move came the added bonus of a one-bedroom flat above the second-rate dining area. Although Tom was the mastermind behind this venture, there was no way in a million years that Big Red would be seen flipping burgers or greeting customers. He approached Nancy and made her an offer she couldn't refuse. She would be the manager of the cafe, with full control of hiring the staff, and she would have the flat above rent-free. If she accepted, then I'd be out on my arse unless I agreed to make the move as well. I had long since vacated my luxury penthouse apartment in Baker Street and was quite content sharing Nancy's lovely flat, located in the picturesque Eldon Square.

Running a cafe would be a big gamble for Nancy, but she took the plunge, knowing that we'd still have a decent income as I would be keeping my job with the famous Otis Reading. She would be giving up a well-paid job at M.E.A.L., a company that calculated advertising expenditure in the media. Her mum also had a part time job at M.E.A.L. I would also be missing out on all the parties that the firm threw, whether it was at Christmas or in the summer, though some of her work colleagues were glad to see the back of me. A few of the girls in particular—Helen, Beverley, and Marion—became slightly nervous when in my company. I can only assume it was to do with a boat trip up the Thames during one such party. Marion foolishly agreed to be my dance partner, so I introduced her to the unique Belfast waltz. After an initial high-velocity spin, she was flung head over heels across the floor into the crowd and then dragged back in again each time she tried to escape. She was finally released after begging for a submission and being close to tears.

McCoy's opened in October 1983. It was named by Tom as a comparison to the Real McCoy name, as he was hoping it would appeal to clientele hankering for a taste of home-cooked fare. The initial kick-off was a pleasant success, with a healthy number of curious patrons on the lookout for something different. There were some snags during the inception, one of them being the kebab debacle. None of us knew how to bind the lamb strips to the rotating spit, resulting in a disaster when most of it fell off and on to the floor. This covert system was obviously buried within the realms of some cult-like inner circle of revolving meat people as no one would offer us any support at all.

Nancy began to build her McCoy's team by employing her mother, Ena, and Eddie's wife, Marie. While these two lovely women had personalities second to none, the fact that they both originally hailed from deepest Glasgow had customers baffled by what language they were speaking.

Ena would be constantly questioning Nancy about the price list.

'How much is a cup of tea pet?' she'd ask.

'You know how much it is, Mum. It's ten pence,' Nancy replied on one occasion.

'But how much is a cup of tea for a little old man?' she'd continue.

'*Still* ten pence, Mum,' answered Nancy as she scurried around the kitchen.

Profits sometimes tended to be cut by more than 50 per cent when Ena made a sandwich. The lump of cheddar that she freely applied would have been enough to feed another six or seven customers.

I'd sometimes help out on Sunday afternoons to give Nancy a break. Who would have thought that working in a cafe could be potentially fatal? On one such occasion, it might have been the case as I prepared some tea and biscuits for an elderly couple that was sitting alone in the cafe. That time of day, the place was quite a popular hangout for the robust Irish labourers trying to recover from a heavy session the night before. Some of these fine chaps tended to be permanently pickled, and on this day, I came face-to-face with an oversized machete-wielding maniac. He was absolutely blootered. From the kitchen, I noticed a swaying silhouette, armed with one of the large cutting knives and trying to help himself to a portion from the crumbling kebab meat stack.

Warily I approached the drunken navvy and softly said, 'Please put the knife down and go back to the other side of the counter.'

He wheeled round to confront me, thrusting his arm forward and leaving the point of the glistening weapon not far from my nose. It was squeaky bum time, and I had to be careful if I wanted to keep a full set of nostrils. I looked right into his bloodshot eyeballs; then in a somewhat sterner voice, I demanded that the swaying beast drop the knife. A cold shaft of sunlight illuminated the countertop, and the clock on the wall made a distinctive *tick, tock, tick, tock.*

Apart from my hefty adversary, the elderly couple sitting motionless at a window table were the only other people in the cafe. It was a high-noon standoff. What was my next move? The thumping of my ever-increasing heartbeat grounded me as I attempted to slowly inch my way back to the kitchen. In a short burst of adrenaline, the show was over. The drunken aggressor lunged forward one step, paused, laughed, then put the knife down and climbed back over the countertop. He staggered out of the cafe and on to the street as if nothing had happened.

Living and working in the cafe was not easy for Nancy and me, and the pressure of everyday life came to a head in various forms of conflict between the two of us. Most of the verbal spats were of my making, and because of this, I had to endure the wrath of Nancy. She had been known to throw things at me in the past, but the cafe seemed to provide her with readily accessible ammunition. Because of the close proximity to the town centre, I found myself coming home later than usual as there always seemed to be somewhere open for a final drink. I'd try to sneak into the bedroom without waking her, but the creaky old wooden staircase sent the pigeons scattering about the loft, and the game would be up. Lurking in the shadows, this dangerous woman would then ambush me with a volley of various items of crockery, usually working her way up from cups and saucers to full-size dinner plates. Even though intoxicated, I was still pretty nimble and managed to escape with minor abrasions.

One particular evening though, I would be hit financially when ducking to avoid a high-flying bottle of HP sauce. The tasty condiment whizzed past my left lug, smashed spectacularly against the ceiling, and splashed in all directions. That resulted in us having to repaint the living room as it was impossible to remove the sticky brown spattering that had stained the surrounding walls. Another night, I was close to losing my life in a situation that could easily have been avoided if only I had kept my mouth shut. On this occasion, I was even later than usual, and when I thought that I'd slipped into the living room undetected, my eyes were dazzled by the illumination of the big light. A ferocious glare halted me in my tracks. Nancy was spitting fire, brandishing a clock, yelling and pointing at the dial.

'It's 2 a.m.! Where have you been? The pubs shut at eleven. I'm going to kill you!' she screamed.

It was a scary sight to behold, and I should have cut my losses and apologised, but I didn't. Foolishly I had to open my big trap.

'You're mad. Look at your mad eyes. Look at your mad Wilson eyes!'

Then she blew. Running directly at me, she flung the clock, hitting me smack on the forehead with so much force that it ricocheted up into the air across the room and down the hallway. I glanced over my shoulder then upgraded a really bad state of affairs to a matter of life and death thanks to my comment.

'Doesn't time fly when you're enjoying yourself?'

Immediately, I knew I was done for, and I fled to seek sanctuary down in the cafe. Seconds later and without warning, my especially enraged partner bounded from the darkness, armed with a kitchen knife in each hand, and went in for the kill. Throwing tables and chairs into her path, I managed to unlock the front door and sprint out on to Kings Road, squealing for help. I didn't stop until I was across the Kennet and halfway up Southampton Street. Following that close call, I made a point of coming home early from then on.

A good night's sleep was hard to come by in the flat. Traffic on Kings Road never stopped during the day, and it seemed to be quite a popular thoroughfare in the evening hours. Most nights, the pigeons playing football in the loft was enough to keep me awake, but at the weekend, a few pints helped me to nod off. Not so on one particular evening. For a chosen few every, Friday was still the boys' night out, though the crowd was gradually dwindling as most of us were now shacked up with the fairer sex. Some of these lovely ladies had firm grasps of their male partners' ball bags, thus preventing any weekend gallivanting. For three of the free birds—Muff, Eugene, and me—it was business as usual, and that night, we'd finished the session off down at the Boars Head. We were standing at the entrance to Smelly Alley, talking shit, before the other two were to head off towards Oxford Road. I had but a short amble through the town centre.

A fish lorry on a late-night delivery had parked beside where we stood, and Muff was in fact leaning against it, having a smoke.

Before we split up, Muff turned to me and said, 'Do you fancy some fish?'

'Aye, all right then,' I said.

In a flash, Muff had grabbed a box of fish from the back of the van. He then summoned Eugene to take an end, and they were off on their heels up Friar Street. I slid a second box from the truck and headed in the other direction to Kings Road. That was it for the evening, so it was off to bed and into the land of Nod in no time.

Everything was well in dreamland until about 5.30 a.m., when Nancy began to yell into my lug, 'Wake up, wake up! There's some nutter screaming and banging at the front door!'

Bloody typical, I thought. My Saturday morning lie-in was out the window.

'Who is it?' I asked.

'I don't know, but if they keep on banging, I'm calling the police,' she replied. Rubbing the sleep from my eyes, I carefully lifted the lower sash window and peeped out at the lunatic below.

'Who is it? What do they want?' enquired Nancy.

I rubbed my eyes again, and shaking my head, I said, 'It's Julie.'

'What does she want?' asked Nancy.

'I don't know, but it must be serious. You better let her come in,' I returned.

Nancy ushered Julie into the living room, and I could hear the anxiety in her voice as I came downstairs from the bedroom. She was shaking all over; then Nancy asked what was wrong.

'Eugene hasn't come home. I don't know where he is,' she said, visibly upset. When I walked into the living room, she began to question me. 'Where's Eugene? Where's Eugene!' she pleaded, demanding an answer.

I scratched my head and tried to recall our last movements.

'Is he with the dirty woman? Did he meet the dirty woman?' continued Julie, voice trembling and completely flustered.

The 'dirty woman' was an attractive older lady that Eugene used to frequent further up in Jesse Terrace, but he'd long been shot of her. I paced the floor, thinking that the horny git had maybe pulled another bit of stuff after the pub. However, I quickly discarded the idea, knowing that he would not do that to Julie. But then again, he *was* with Muff. My mind was all over the show, and it was hard to think with Julie howling like a banshee. I went into the kitchen to get some water, and as I gulped the glass dry, I noticed something on the countertop. It was a box of frozen fish. Then the pieces of the jigsaw began to fall into place. The dopey bastards had probably been lifted by the police.

Giggling to myself, I returned to join the girls.

Julie asked, 'Why are you laughing?'

'I think I know where Eugene is, maybe in jail,' I said.

'Thank God for that. He's not with another woman,' she wept joyfully.

199

It seemed that Julie was relieved to find out that Eugene was in jail as opposed to dirty dogging it, so she up and left.

The next day, my thoughts turned out to be correct. Both of them were in the clink. They'd sneaked through the back streets, trying to lie low, and were stopped by a patrol car and then carted off to the cells. I, on the other hand, had walked right past the late-night revellers down through the town centre and home. By the afternoon, they were still locked up. Muff was scheduled to turn out for our football team, and Melinda had the scissors ready to cut his shirt and shorts to ribbons. She thought the same as Julie—that he was with another woman. These girls had no faith in their honourable men. They would have been released hours before but for Eugene's stubbornness.

Muff was worried about not being able to play football the following day and had admitted 'It was a fair cop, guv' almost immediately, but Eugene would not be broken. He held firm to their original, absolutely unbelievable story that they both had concocted. Whilst Muff sat patiently in his cell, awaiting emancipation, a police sergeant and constable were engaged in a battle of attrition with his pal. The interrogation went something like this:

Police constable	Where did you get the fish from?
Eugene	We bought it from a big black man in the Boars Head.
Police sergeant	For God's sake, Mr McCartan! You've been here all night man—it's 1 p.m. now. Just tell me where you got the fish! Your friend Mr Smith has already confessed.
Eugene	From a big black man in the Boars Head.
Police constable	You're trying to tell me that a black chap approached you in the pub and undid his coat to reveal a twenty-five-pound box of coley saithe on his person? He was dealing fish? For the last time, *where did you get the fish?*'
Eugene	From a big black man in the Boars Head.

Police sergeant	But your mate has already told us that you nicked it from the back of a lorry parked outside Smelly Alley.
Eugene	I'm not falling for the good cop–bad cop routine. Muff would never squeal. We bought it from a big black man in the Boars Head.

The exhausted police officers retreated, beaten and unable to crack their obstinate adversary. Ultimately, he did break but not before the officers had taken early leave due to mental exhaustion. Muff missed the first ten minutes of the game, which ended in a 2–2 draw. I scored a last-minute spectacular horizontal scissor kick to salvage a point, and Muff was absolutely average.

After the notorious fish caper, the cafe thrived with an almost 100 percent profit from the daily lunchtime special: fish and chips. A lot of cops enjoyed the cut-price fare and were culpable in the mystery of the missing fish as well as assisting in the disposal of the evidence by eating it. The special angling unit of the Thames Valley Police had trawled the back streets of Reading for two missing boxes of coley saithe, casting their lines far and wide. Affiliates of the seedy underworld were questioned in an attempt to catch anyone dealing second-hand fish to any unsuspecting members of the public. Even the FBI (Fish Bandit Investigators) got involved.

Muff and Eugene had one box confiscated by the local bobbies, and I had the other, so who had nabbed the third? The answer was apparent by the amount of fish suppers we had been selling at the cafe. When I hoisted the slippery morsels on to my shoulder from the back of the ghost truck, I had been in fact making off with a double box. By November, half of the Reading populace would be accessories in crime by dining at our establishment.

The ill-gotten gains went a long way towards a new car and a Christmas holiday on the beach. We would swap the cold and grey skies of Berkshire for a dose of the sun in the tourist town of Agadir in southern Morocco.

CHAPTER 23

RED HEELS IN THE SAHARA

Like Lord and Lady Muck, Nancy and I headed off to join the elite in a five-star resort on the sandy shores of the Atlantic coast via a stop-off in Casablanca. We figured that landing in the famed city of Humphrey Bogart and Ingrid Bergman would surely enhance the romanticism and intrigue, as we imagined that we would feel as if we were entering a smoke-hazed film set. It did nothing of the sort.

The plane literally hit the runway in Casablanca during a monsoon, making us feel that our decision to fly off to an exotic climate had been a slightly dubious one. The young pilot and co-pilot handled the landing as if it was their first time in a cockpit. The dated Air Morocco turbo prop did not seem to slow as it battled a full-blown storm and bounced on to the tarmac before skidding violently. Overhead compartments burst open, scattering the handheld cases about the compact fuselage. Cries of anguish filled the air in English, French, Arabic, and maybe a dialect of Klingon as each passenger prayed to their particular god. After what felt like an eternity, the plane finally jerked to a halt, cushioned by a grass verge after it had careered sideways out of control. Stunned passengers later huddled in the airport lounge in silence, realising how lucky they'd been. You could have cut the tension with a knife when the broadcaster later announced that the connecting flight to Agadir was ready to board.

Eventually, we did arrive safely at the lavish resort, where we were greeted by blazing sunshine and smiling staff members. The town was abuzz with activity, which was centred round the enormous bazaar, complete with jugglers and merchandisers haggling for a trade. We embraced the hypnotic atmosphere as we wandered in and out of each stall, soaking up the impressive sideshows as the stall owners went about their business.

One extravagant merchant dressed in a Tommy Cooper hat and a bright pair of marzipan-coloured tartan trousers had an oversized jacket on my back in an instant.

'You buy jacket, eighty pounds, real antelope,' he said.

'Clear aff, I don't want your jacket,' I replied.

'Twenty pounds,' he returned, dropping sixty pounds in a trice.

I bid the Moroccan Billy Connelly adieu and hastily made off before he tried to sell me any mountain goat attire.

The resort catered generously to each vacationer. One could be pampered in a high-class sauna and spa or take in a talent show while eating a delicious meal, then relax by the pool while being tended to by glamorous staff members. This was fine and dandy for us as we'd never experienced anything upmarket before, but we were young and easily bored.

The real adrenaline rush was to be had outside the lavish complex, where one could mingle with the eccentric locals. One-eyed snake charmers and shady characters performing adroit acts while lying on beds of nails were particularly appealing. Paddling in the Atlantic Ocean for the first time was a stunning experience, as we inhaled the salty aroma that came wafting in off the vast body of endless water. Nevertheless, we were wise enough to adhere to the warning signs that we saw posted at various locations along the waterfront.

Threatening posters advising tourists to steer clear of the beach during the evening hours 'for fear of death' and an illustration depicting a throat slicing action was enough to limit our out-and-about activities to the daytime. On one such walk along the sandy shore, we happened upon a Bedouin offering camel rides. As we were the only souls on the beach at that time, he seemed desperate to make a sale and immediately dropped the going rate by ten dinars. As it was to be our first-ever ride on this specific type of beast of burden, we were a bit apprehensive about mounting the side-mouth-chewing, gob-spitting creature, which also had a dose of perpetual flatulence. It knelt to allow us access to its strong back and craggy hump and then rose to take us higher up than it had initially looked from the ground. Just before boarding the animal, its handler removed Nancy's handbag from her grasp, causing her some concern.

'He's taken my bag!' she exclaimed, obviously worried that he might hike up his skirts and be off with his ill-gotten gains.

With a calm reassurance, I replied: 'Don't worry. We've got his camel!'

Although at times slightly irresponsible, we both kept a low profile and abided by the rules of the land and stayed safe. One day though, we pushed our luck a bit too far. I thought we should get out of town to see what the real Morocco looked like, and to do this, we had to rent a car. Enter two naive mugs who made off to the Southern Sahara in a clunky old Renault Four minus air conditioning. Along the dusty trails, we witnessed stalls selling fly-infested carcasses hanging on hooks, and others offering up rotten forms of vegetables. Men squatting by the roadside to have a shit seemed to be common practice. We had been following signs for La Plage, but as we ventured onwards, they all but disappeared. I pulled over to a store at the next village to ask for directions to the nearest beach.

Upon returning to the car, I found a distraught Nancy folded over inside, covering her legs from a gaggle of local hissing women and horny men frothing at the mouth.

'Clear aff ya dirty bastards!' I yelled, and luckily for me, there was a scattering match as they scurried back into their holes in the ground.

Needless to say, anytime I tried to ask for help, no one had any clue what I was saying. Whether my high school French in a Belfast accent was impossible to understand or we were just being given the cold shoulder, I don't know. One thing was certain, though: we were on our own. Blindly I kept on driving. For the most part, the road was pretty rough, but eventually, I noticed a gradual change as it began to feel smoother and we began to slow down. It was not a good thing.

The car became sluggish, and it became difficult to control the speed or steering. An unpleasant burning smell was apparent, and the overheating light was glowing on the dashboard, so I thought it wise to trundle to a halt. I opened the bonnet to try to cool the engine down and let the steam evaporate. Nancy exited and offered me a drink of warm water from the only bottle we had left as the blistering heat increased.

Leaning against the car, dazzled by the intense sunlight, I scanned the area and realised there was no sign of a road behind, in front of, or at any side of us. There was nothing but sand as far as the eye could see. We were lost in the desert! Using all my survival skills, I summoned Nancy to get back into the car and then panicked. I cranked the engine over and began driving aimlessly. The only thing we had in our favour was that we had plenty of fuel, but without water or air conditioning, we would soon be cooked.

After half an hour of our struggling wheel-deep in sand dunes, the future looked bleak. I had no idea of what to do as we seemed to be going deeper and deeper into the mighty Sahara. It was pointless to get out and walk as there was nothing on the horizon to head towards apart from sand dune after sand dune. Our hiking apparel was not exactly suited for a brisk walk across an endless desert. I was clad in a heavy navy-blue Scotland football shirt, and Nancy had dressed prepared for battling the silky sands of time in tight shorts and red stiletto heels. We just kept on driving.

Just as we were about to give up and let the elements get the better of us, a vehicle appeared in the distance. As it neared, we could clearly see a driver and a passenger of a pick-up truck, with two other men in the back. They had the look of menacing bandits. Our heartbeats increased as the truck drew up alongside; then the driver gestured with his hand that we should follow them. We had no option but to follow; if we stayed any longer, exposed to the heat, we would surely be goners.

'We've got to go with them,' I said worriedly.

'But where are they taking us?' replied Nancy. 'They might murder me and rape you,' she said with a nervous grin.

Following a twenty-minute drive, a ranch-type building could be seen up ahead. As we approached the entranceway, a large set of double gates opened, and we followed the truck into an open courtyard. Our anxiety increased as we watched the large gates close behind us; then a handful of inhabitants gathered on the overhead verandas, unsure of what they were witnessing.

This is it, I thought. Surely we would soon be sliced up a treat.

One of the banditos leaped from the back of the truck and paced towards our car. We quickly wound up the windows and locked the doors, although it seemed futile as we were sure our demise was imminent. He turned his back and pointed to a second set of gates that slowly opened.

Then he indicated that we should go on through. Was that the place where we would be tortured and burnt alive? I eased the car through the opening into the unknown, where I merged on to a fully lined highway with signposts to Agadir. It was full speed ahead back to the car rental, then into the sanctuary of the resort, where we stayed for the rest of the week, never venturing beyond the safety of its grounds. Who needs culture?

After another anxious flight on the way home, it was back to reality, burgers and inadequate kebabs at the cafe, as we began to try to make a profit in order to prepare for our next holiday. By the next summer though, it was all over bar the shouting. No one told us that fewer people fed their faces in the summer than they did in the winter months. Within less than a year, the cafe closed, thus leaving the rats and pigeons to fend for themselves. We were now homeless, but it seemed right that the next move would be to buy a house instead of renting.

CHAPTER 24

THE SPANISH EXPEDITION

Nancy had been taken back by M.E.A.L., and I was still working at Otis, but we scarcely had two bob to rub together between us. Overlooking the small necessity of not having any money, we went ahead and bought our first house in Tidmarsh Street. This would not have been possible if it wasn't for an eccentric bin-head lawyer friend of Tom's who lent us 1,500 pounds but forgot to ask for it back. We also forgot to remind him.

Too bad, so sad, we thought.

In spite of our financial difficulties, we managed to survive and run our neat semi-detached home on a thin budget, though there was a lot of stress and anxiety in doing so. During our time there, we had countless parties and various interlopers. Michael stayed in between his final Arabian adventure and setting up a bar in Spain, and Jimmy Humphries, a friend of mine from Belfast, became a long-term lodger. He had recently returned from Australia and was now aimlessly wandering about England in search of new horizons and asked if he could stay for a week or so. Eugene christened him Jimmy Washing Machine, a name derived from the band Jimmy the Hoover.

Having unexpected lodgers put a lot of strain on Nancy and me, and we feuded quite a lot throughout that period. Although our home in Tidmarsh Street was larger than an average house for first-time buyers, the street itself was not great. A fruit-and-vegetable warehouse was located directly behind us, and the 5.30 a.m. loading-up time had us wakened by noisy truck engines and loud, foul-mouthed workers. We needed to move. Within nine months, we would sell up and make a profit of 8,000 pounds to put down as a nice deposit on our next house in Beecham Road. We got the all-clear to move in on the first week of August. It would be a new start, and it would surely ease the tension between us. Best-laid plans and all that.

One fine day in July during our annual trip to the Henley Regatta, the bad blood spilled over into total hostility. I had been in a pretty obnoxious mood before and during the event, which was attended by quite a few of our regular friends. As usual, a lot of drink and illicit substances began to flow, and I became all the more disorderly. The Regatta was a yearly showpiece for the upper-class toffs, but we went because of the exceptional beer tent. Nancy had warned me to cool down on numerous occasions, but I was like a runaway train that would inevitably crash and self-destruct. My head was filled with broken bottles, and badness began to flow through my veins.

After one final warning, Nancy left with some other people and instructed me that if I didn't get my act together, then I should not come back home. Like a fool, I ignored her and kept on drinking as a way to continue my act of defiance, indulging in various forms of nuisance and degeneracy. At some point in the evening, my system eventually shut down, and my head caved in. The next morning, I woke up in Muff's flat, feeling sick to my stomach, and had no idea of how we'd managed to get back alive. When I finally did go home, I found a note saying it was over. Nancy had cleared off.

There was a limited amount of communication between us during the next few days, but that was not an unusual result after we had slapped each other about. It was different this time though. Nancy felt that we had grown so far apart that we would be unable to reconcile our differences; we both seemed to want different things in life. I did not wish to split, but I also thought we could not make the relationship work so maybe she was right. Now it was just Jimmy Washing Machine and myself.

The sale of the house in Tidmarsh Street was finalised, so we both had to get out. As for Nancy and me, the new property was ready for the takeover. However, as we were on the verge of a break-up, we had to come to some kind of agreement on what to do next. We decided to split whatever profit we had made on Tidmarsh Street and then go our own ways. The bank was to give us two separate cheques, and I was to take on the mortgage of the new house and move in alone. Nancy would move back to her parents' house and start over again.

Three of her brothers rallied around to help cheer her up by carrying out a most unusual plan. Tom, John, and Stuart decided that a little excursion to Spain to see Michael at his bar would be just the tonic she needed. While the trip in itself was not unusual, the fact that Tom was going along certainly was. People joked that this event would surely soon make front page news headlines in the *Reading Evening Post*. Tom had never flown before. He very rarely left the Reading area. If he did venture from the vicinity of the town, it was typically against his will and the scratch marks on the signposts could attest to that. So while Nancy was sunning herself in Benalmadena, Jimmy Washing Machine and I completed the long, hard slog of moving stuff from Tidmarsh Street to Beecham Road.

During that sortie to Spain, the four Wilson siblings were to learn a few things about each other that they had not previously known. As it was Tom's first time on an airplane, he was made aware that beer would be brought directly to the seat rather than him going to the bar to get one. Stuart was begrudgingly entertained each night when he was awakened to discover that one of his brothers had a sleep-enhancing dance routine. John would run on the spot, then bounce about the room with his fingers raised, singing, 'Tommy, Tommy, Tommy.' During this strange ritual, he would sporadically lunge forward with an outstretched digit and would then press it against the tip of Stuart's nose.

There was also an agreement between the siblings that a serious intervention was needed so that they could discuss Stuart's malodorous feet. The disgusting, unbearable stench emitted from his foul plates could potentially have damaged the scent glands of anyone in close proximity. This unanimous consensus was reached one evening after

Stuart had strategically placed an odour eater from one of his shoes inside Tom's pillowcase. The mysterious pong had Tom holding his nose throughout the night, thus depriving him of any sleep at all. They all agreed that in the future, Stuart should only remove his shoes when no one else was anywhere near him.

When the Wilsons returned from Spain, I phoned Nancy as I thought the few weeks away might have changed things between us. She still did not want to move back in with me, but we were a lot more civil to each other than we were before the Spanish expedition. Over the next few weeks, we would go out together but still kept our distance. Rather than going out with the lads each week, I thought that I should treat Nancy to a night at the cinema or take her out for a meal as I hoped that this tactic might help ease some of the uncertainty between us.

Otis Reading had booked the Lakeside Country Club in Frimley for a company bonding session, and I was allocated four tickets. We were to see the *guv'nor* Bob Monkhouse in action. He was known mainly for his family-themed game shows, such as *The Golden Shot* and *Bob's Full House*. But when he was on the stage as a stand-up comedian, his act could be quite risqué. This was the kind of event in an upscale club that I was sure that Nancy would enjoy, and if I was on my best behaviour, then who knew? The place was sold out, so the company had really gone out of their way to offer us some high-end entertainment. Nancy and I had two of the tickets, and I asked Eugene and Julie if they would like to join us as our guests.

The club was amazing. Strobe lights mounted high on the ceiling filtered across the main hall to complement the plush carpets and a comfortable dining set-up. Rows of tables that seated ten people flanked the stage, with the left section slightly lower to provide an excellent vantage point. My company had booked two of the tables on the right side, so we had to step up to be seated. I ushered Nancy and my guests to their seats, ready to relish in the finer aspects of a congenial night out. I was acting like an adult now. What could go wrong?

We settled in, soaking up the atmosphere and enjoying a few drinks before the meals were served. Bob had the audience in the palm of his hand as they hung on to every one-liner and blue joke that he delivered.

It was wise to stay seated during his act as the master of wit was quick to seize upon anyone strolling around and proceed to tear them to pieces. A few pints later, I was busting for a lash, but the thought of getting up terrified me as I would certainly crumble under Mr Monkhouse's roasting. It was no good though; I could not hold it in any longer.

I glanced at the table opposite to see a merry group of older people in fine form, some of them giggling as they watched their freshly lit glasses of sambuca give off a distinct blue flame.

This is my chance, I thought. *Maybe the little fire show might distract Bob enough to let me slide off to the toilet totally unnoticed.* I then made my move and edged stealthily past the others at the table, taking slow but deliberate strides. *So far so good,* I thought. *He hasn't spotted me.*

All I had to do was ease out into the passageway between the two sets of tables, and I'd be off to the races without Bob noticing. My efficient final manoeuvre would have been one step to shelter had it not been for the height difference between the two table arrays. My body shifted forward as my foot struggled to find the floor. The momentum flung me into the air, and I swan-dived across the opposite table, scattering beers, martinis, and an assortment of flaming tipples. As I slithered the complete table length on my belly, I had just enough time to observe the wide-eyed open-mouthed group sitting motionless as I passed on by. The look of horror and disgust on the faces of the bewildered ten was a sight to behold. I crumpled to a halt when my head crashed against the side wall, and I was up and out of there in milliseconds.

Thankfully, Mr Monkhouse missed my skydiving act, but I was not very popular with the neighbours sitting opposite. I returned to an extremely irate group, some dripping wet, others smouldering from the after-effects of flying lagers and smoking sambucas. Maybe an apology would have helped a little.

Nancy had a good time that night, and she did not seem to mind my high-flying act. We were getting along better than ever, and although living in separate houses had a lot to do with it, there was a chance that we could try again—for a third time. When I promised to take an oath to be a good boy, Nancy gave me a favourable nod. We agreed to give it another go, so she transferred her share from the sale of Tidmarsh

Street into the Northern Rock Building Society and became the joint owner of 141 Beecham Road.

Firstly, I had to deal with a sticky issue that involved two washing machines. Nancy suggested that she did not need both and chose the one that could wash clothes automatically; so unfortunately for Jimmy, he had to go.

CHAPTER 25

HEATHENS TO THE RIGHT

By 1984 the close-knit crowd of people that I spent every weekend with was slowly evolving and maturing as they each met their matches. One couple would buy a house, and then in no time at all, we'd all have one. We were just following the instructions in the manual that had been left by previous generations, and now our time had come.

Sadly, it was the year that we lost one of the all-time comedy greats: Tommy Cooper. He had died in front of a mass live television audience during one of his skits. In other news, the pound note disappeared, and a group of musicians banded together to raise funds for famine relief in Ethiopia by recording 'Do They Know It's Christmas?' Unfortunately, Bucks Fizz had everybody 'Talking in Their Sleep'; Phil Collins was still singing 'Against All Odds'; 'Robert De Niro's Waiting' on Bananarama; and Russ Abbot created a strange 'Atmosphere'.

Beaker had returned from Spain and was awaiting the arrival of his Swedish girlfriend, Nina, whom he'd met whilst working at Michael's bar in Benalmadena. There were rumblings about the possibility of a future wedding. If the Beak was thinking of marriage, then what chance did the rest of us have? And sure enough, Steve proposed; then we were all at it. When the big day came, Steve married Anne in the large chapel on the Tilehurst Road. This was the first time that I had attended a service in a Catholic church, and astonishingly, I had lived to tell the tale. No lightning bolts, floods, or plagues. What was really handy about the wedding was that the reception was held in a hall which was attached to the church, so there was no poncing about in cars or taxis after the service.

Anne's family were all Irish Catholics and Steve's were all Scottish heathens. Following the priest's proclamation that they were husband and wife, he indicated that if anyone required Holy Communion, they should line up and approach the altar. Anne's lot had been sitting on the left side of the church, and they gracefully rose, bowed their heads, and formed an orderly queue. Steve's lot, sitting on the right side, boisterously rose, cleared off, and formed a chaotic queue at the bar. By the time the Catholics took their places in the hall, the heathens had drunk all the beer.

Not long after, Eugene and Julie made their vows at the same venue, arriving in semi-style in a white Rolls Royce. The lack of a full set of hubcaps troubled a very miffed Marcus, who had provided the Roller as his wedding present. On seeing that the keys were left in the ignition, I seized the moment and slid into the Silver Lady's plush leather seats; I then started her, much to the chagrin of the disgruntled chauffeur. Eugene's aunt and I came up with a clever prank to use some nurse's tape to send out a secretive distress call. We took advantage of another Catholic wedding by carrying out the old caper of sticking 'HELP' in bright shiny letters to the soles of his shoes as he knelt at the altar. This resulted in a jolly good chortle from within the audience. Each of these weddings at the splendid church lasted as long as a football match, but it was worth it to see the handsome grooms and the beautiful brides. Up next was the Croft–Wilson wedding.

The chances of Nancy and me surviving in holy matrimony for more than two years had the bookmakers holding steady with the odds of 100–1 for anyone that fancied a flutter. Our relationship up to that point had been very volatile, with Nancy being the volatile part of it. So based on that steady but precarious foundation, I suggested that we should get married, and Nancy nodded in a way that I took for granted was a yes. Later at the altar, she nudged me to show an engagement ring that she had perhaps found in an apple pie, reminding me that we'd somehow skipped that bit. We had been living in Beecham Road for over a year before we set the date for our big day. A nearby picturesque Anglican church in the Tilehurst Road seemed to be the perfect venue to get married, so we approached the minister to see if he would do the deed.

Upon hearing that neither Nancy nor I had been christened, he looked upon us as if we were children of Satan and shooed us away. He was without doubt a charming twat of the cloth indeed.

We decided to get thee hence from there, but as we were nearly hence, the learned man of God spake on to us, 'I could fit you into our flock for a sum of seventy-five pounds.'

In reply, I said verily on to he, 'You can flock off and stick your church up your arse!'

We searched in vain at various locations, but no one would bless our union. Finally, a short, fat, bald, scooter-riding vicar took up the challenge and offered his services at a small Methodist church in Tilehurst. The reception would be in the community centre across the road, providing that the teenybopper disco wasn't on that night.

With a limited budget, we foolishly arranged everything ourselves, including organising the catering and obtaining a liquor license so that we could ultimately supply the alcoholic beverages along with the bar staff. We even rented the glasses. John and Stuart had opened up their own off-license, the very successful Grog Shop, so we got a bit of a deal on the beer, wine, and spirits. The first mistake was storing the alcohol in the garage of our house. I had planned to stay with Eugene and Julie the night before the wedding as our place was filled up with family members over from Belfast. Nancy had already arranged to stay at her mum's house. My two uncles, John and Tom, were partial to the odd nip now and then, so being the great host that I was, I left them the key to the oversized liquor cabinet. It was the second mistake, and it was a costly one.

'You can have a couple of drinks if you want, but make sure you lock the garage when you're done,' I explained.

The next morning, I arrived at the house bright and early so that I could get dressed for the wedding. Everyone was still in bed, apart from my two uncles, who hadn't made it that far. The living room had empty bottles strewn about the floor. Uncle John and Tom were clocked out, the latter on the sofa and the other slumped over a chair. In one short evening, they had polished off the entire Guinness collection. It was an exceptionally fine start to the day.

Beaker was my best man and seemed to have everything under control, so I wasn't overly worried about any major disasters occurring. At one point, he even averted a break and enter. None of our glasses had turned up, and Beaker was able to hold me back from smashing in the doors of the Glass Mountain, the place that was meant to be supplying them. The owner had gone missing. He was tracked down, and after some gentle intimidation in his shell-like, he was persuaded to get his finger out and deliver the glasses. I was now somewhat settled and ready for a stiff drink before the ceremony.

The weather that day in July was good for a wedding, which merely meant that it wasn't raining. Most people met in the nearby Plough, a pub that had a beer garden. There were a few police officers hovering around, questioning passers-by. A notice pinned to the door of the pub informed those who entered that a man had been stabbed on the premises the previous night. He had since died, so it was now a murder enquiry. There was an air of unease amongst the local patrons, so most of the wedding contingent did not overstay their welcome, instead choosing to leave after a couple of swift ones.

Next stop was the church, to participate in Budget Weddings Limited. The hall was filled as the guests awaited the arrival of the bride and her bridesmaids. Eventually, the gleaming white wedding car arrived, adorned with splendid ribbons, and the chauffeur escorted the bridal party to the church entrance. He was in fact Neil, driving his newly acquired company car (a Ford Sierra) and eager to play his part in Budget Weddings Limited. Nancy was radiant as she marched up the aisle into the unknown, as were her two assistants: her niece Lucy and my niece, the enchanting wee Corinne.

Unlike your average wedding, we exchanged vows, did the kiss thing, and then headed into the back room, where we signed the books and were up the aisle and out the door before anyone could raise an objection. One of our crowd, Richard, was the rare owner of a video camera, and set up his equipment to record the speeches and cake cutting. That way, as the years rolled by, we would have a keepsake that we would be able to pull out any time we were feeling nostalgic. We were presented with seven minutes of footage that cut out abruptly just as I rose to deliver the speech that I had been preparing for over a month. According to Richard, it was due to technical difficulties, but it was mainly because his camera was *crap*!

The early evening festivities went well, with everyone boogying on down, apart from Nancy. She had been wearing contact lenses throughout the day for a much-longer period than she was used to. They had become an irritant and began to impair her vision, so she sneaked into the bathroom to remove them. The lenses had adhered tight, and she tore a film off her eyeballs when attempting to slide the lenses away, leaving her virtually blind. She was in a panic and consulted my cousin Colin, an optician, who treated her briefly with some soothing lotions.

Even though Nancy was suffering, we still managed to squeeze in a romantic dance to our chosen wedding song 'Romeo and Juliet' by Dire Straits. Her evening was now all but shot, and she asked if we could go on to Pangbourne to retire to our bridal suite at the Copper Inn. Considering we had an early start the next morning, I thought it was a wise idea, so we bid our guests farewell, leaving them all to have a grand old time. We were travelling to Cephalonia, one of the Greek islands, for a two-week honeymoon.

Nancy spent the rest of the evening lying on the bed and wearing sunglasses to protect her eyes from the painful light. I did her no favours as I described how the beautiful room was ornately decorated, with roses and bridal ribbons scattered on top of the four-poster bed. Her headache went into overdrive during my review of the riverside window table, which was garnished with succulent appetizers spread liberally on a silver platter. It pained me to listen to her suffering as I polished off the veritable snacks and washed them down with a few flutes of Moét & Chandon. In my defence, I was eating for two.

Dressed like Jackie Onassis, Nancy struggled on to the airplane, though she was given disability status as she grasped my arm while boarding. It certainly sped the whole procedure up. We had put our name down for a last-minute cancellation, and although it meant sharing a villa with another couple, it was a real bargain at a third of the original price. As we flew through the clouds, a shiver ran down my spine as I pictured two fat sweaty old bastards awaiting our arrival at the villa. I could see them picking their noses and arseholes, farting and burping and constantly creating the ambience of a pig farm.

It was a searing thirty degrees Celsius when we landed at the small airport: the perfect temperature to enhance bad smells in an enclosed area. It had been a particularly long and uncomfortable flight for Nancy, who was still unable to see and missing out on the beautiful scenic island. Both knackered, we didn't care what kind of flatmates awaited us; we just wanted to clock out on a bed.

The picturesque villa was much more than we expected. It was nestled back in a cosy lemon grove, with stunning views of the harbour. That was not the only thing that was eye-catching. I had been keeping Nancy updated about what the surrounding landscape looked like, hoping that her sight would soon return. We were welcomed at the entrance of the villa by the pair that we would be intimately spending the next two weeks with.

I took one step back and gulped. *What a pair!*

There in front of our eyes (well, my eyes) were two beautiful young girls, one topless. I gulped again.

Nancy then asked, 'Are you going to introduce me then?'

'Hello, this is Nancy, and I am Alan,' I said, offering my hand.

'Hello, I'm Lisa, and this is my younger sister, Mandy,' said the one with the tits out.

Nancy seemed relieved that we hadn't been shacked up with the kind of sweaty bastards I had envisioned in my daydream, although she had no idea that one of the girls had her kit off. That night I almost joined Nancy in the blind department as the older sister strutted around the villa semi-clad. Later she would be completely stark bollock naked, covering herself occasionally with a diminutive towel following a shower. Alas, all things must pass. Nancy's sight returned the next morning, but I could have lost mine had my new wife carried out her threat of poking my eyes out if I kept looking in the wrong direction.

For the remainder of the holiday, life in the villa was a mixture of relaxation and trepidation. On one hand, I'd kick back on the patio and soak up the rays whilst peeling myself the odd lemon that fell from our own personal grove. At other times, I'd be dodging uppercuts from my beautiful bride as I rubbernecked the sparsely clothed sisters as they passed from room to room. To make things worse, the two young girls insisted that they should join us each day at the beach, and as hard as I tried to dissuade them, they just would not take no for an answer.

When we did shake them off, it was still no easier for me. Cephalonia was a bit of an unknown source for tourists, and it had just recently opened its doors to the people of the UK. Up until then, for some reason, the Finnish had been the only nationals to enjoy the beautiful island, and we all know what Scandinavians are like. On one beach, we found ourselves in the midst of what seemed to be a gathering only for beautiful blonde youths, and swimwear was definitely optional. As we found a spot amongst an array of large-breasted splendour, these bathing beauties seemed genuinely shocked that we were partially clothed. This time Nancy accepted that tits out was a natural state at this sandy Shangri-La, but it was difficult to disregard the girls lying with legs akimbo. Later I thought that I was doing the right thing by taking various shots of Nancy emerging from the surf. That was until the film was developed. The glamorous wet look poses and stunning scenery were not enough to disguise the naked Finns strategically positioned in the background.

The evening hours were a much easier affair, as everyone was fully clothed. We got to know a few English sunseekers. They were easy to spot because of their beetroot burnt faces and their awkward gait, a by-product of their scorched feet. As usual, it was a race to see who could get as much ouzo down their necks in the shortest possible time. It was a race that I won handsomely. During the telling of an overextended joke to a couple from Leeds and a couple from Stroud, I collapsed on to the table, scattering glasses and bottles. In the aftermath of my subsidence, I'd managed to get barred from all the cab companies in town and in a fallout with our newfound friends.

While the taxi rank incident was totally my fault, Nancy pissed the drunken Brits off by telling them that our villa was close by. The two-mile hike carrying my comatose shell up a steep hill was enough to end a brief but interesting friendship. We spent the last week quietly exploring the cultural aspects of the island, visiting some of the beautiful churches and museums. In one such establishment, we found a strange display of the skeletal remains of Saint Andrew's left foot in a glass case. On the final day, we hung out at Lord Byron's house, but he wasn't home.

Before heading back home, we had to endure a sweaty and sticky wait at the small airport as the flight was delayed for over an hour. There was no refreshment lounge to buy food or drink from, just one compact room with plastic seats, and this left the passengers hot and irritable. Wasps and flies buzzed around our heads to make the wait even more unpleasant. Kids yapped, and their mothers swore as the temperature rose. The uneasy tension was finally broken when it was announced that the plane at last was now ready to board.

Beside the main door to the runway, an older man wearing a kilt calmly packed away his book and reached down to a small case at his feet. Without batting an eyelid, he whipped out a set of bagpipes and began to march out on to the tarmac to the tune of 'Scotland the Brave'. We, along with the other passengers, joined in behind him to form a jubilant line and proceeded to march across the tarmac. The relief was plain to see as everyone climbed up the stairway to take their seats. It was the perfect way for Nancy and me to end an eventful honeymoon.

The budget wedding was to end up quite expensive when all the smoke had cleared. As we had taken off to Greece while the reception was in full swing, no one had informed us of how the evening played out. There had been a big scrap between a boyfriend and girlfriend, a couple who spent their spare time *not* fighting, which had resulted in some walls being bashed in. Donald, our head barman, decided to try to collect all the glasses in one lift and proceeded to drop them, and someone busted a toilet door. The Reading Borough Council handed us a bill of 250 pounds at a double-time charge to repair the damages because, in their extreme wisdom, they decided that it had to be done on a Sunday. We lost the deposit on the rental glasses plus an extra charge for extreme breakage. Apart from that, the evening was a huge success, with everyone except the two jilted lovebirds having a fun-filled time.

The weddings just kept on coming with Dave and Jacqui taking the plunge, followed by Stef and Binders, Greg and Julia, Simon and Alison, Nick and Ness, Stuart and Mary and then Pete and Sue.

Although they cost a lot of money, these unions brought us all together under the same roof, where we let all our inhibitions hang out and acted like we had in the days of old. These times were slowly dwindling as each of the crowd naturally spent more time with their respective partners. Also, some had left the area for good. Brian had cleared off to California, and my old mate Beaker married Nina in Reading before choosing to establish their family in her native Sweden. Simon was later to depart for Australia with his new girl, Stephanie. Stuart and John had sold the Grog shop in Reading and opened up its namesake in Oxford, where they both chose to reside.

The days of twenty or so of us meeting for a rare old time at the weekend were over. The gatherings were limited to a two-hour lunchtime session in the pub on a Sunday afternoon, but that also halted when the screaming brats arrived. First one appeared, and then everyone began to begat. A few short years before, it would have been laughable to think that any of us could be mature enough to become a parent, but we did. Not only that, but most members of the group that had once lit up Reading with their buffoonery and high jinks would later raise children to be proud of.

Nancy and I had two boys in quick succession, Sam and Bobby. I can't speak for the others on how they felt when they initially became fathers, but for me, it was beyond words. During the nine months that Nancy was pregnant, the uncertainty of what would happen next was always on my mind. I knew everything would change, but I could not envisage how it would be. At that time, I was working in Bristol and had emergency phone numbers located throughout the city. I was ready for the 100-mile-per-hour race back down the M4. My nerves were wrecked by a series of false alarms. This baby did not want to come out.

Finally, the natal doctor decided that he should go in and encourage the little bugger to emerge. A date was chosen for Nancy to be induced, therefore easing my stress about being away and missing the birth. When the labour started, it would be a long struggle in the ward by her bedside. Multiple *Daily Mail* crosswords were completed, and various LPs were played before the wee man chose to make his entry into the world. He was born during the Rolling Stones album *Goats Head Soup* and to the song '100 Years Ago'. Nancy had suffered long and hard to free this little creature, and when he arrived, my mind seemed to leave my body as I experienced a feeling unlike anything before or since. He was born at 7.13 p.m. on 1 September 1986, and by 9 p.m., I was in the Butler, knocking back my fourth pint and celebrating with everyone that I'd phoned. On my way to the pub, I spotted Simon's van parked outside a posh Spanish restaurant. He was in the middle of a romantic date, sitting cosily at a window table.

I abandoned my car, rushed across the street, sidestepping traffic, and burst through the main doorway. With a very arrogant stance and feeling as if I was the only person who had ever become a father, I yelled out, 'Nancy has just had a boy!'

I was gone in an instant, much to the bemusement of the baffled diners. Simon kissed his little lady on the cheek and then was off on his toes, leaving a bewildered woman awaiting an order for two. Later, down at the bar, he presented me with a massive cigar that had been kept in cold storage in anticipation of this special occasion. Simon was a good mate, all right. The rest of the evening was an overdose of euphoria.

The next morning, I was awakened by the twanging of a very badly tuned guitar that I had been cuddling tightly. Stef had talked me into having a couple of nightcaps back at his house after the pub had closed. The surreal evening had concluded when he clocked out, and I picked up his dusty guitar to strum a serenade to the rest of the street during my short walk home.

From that morning on, life took a dramatic shift as I was now a father without a clue. There was more to come as seventeen months later, my second son, Bobby, arrived. His birth was a totally different affair. Nancy felt that the time had come as her waters broke, and she began having severe pains, so we packed a bag and drove to the Royal Berkshire Hospital. Upon the early morning arrival, we were told by the fat midwife on duty that Nancy was imagining things.

Nancy then pleaded for help and exclaimed that the baby was coming out and that she could feel her legs being pushed apart.

To this, fatty replied, 'If you would have kept your legs closed nine months ago, you would not be in this predicament.'

She then ushered us into a small, dingy, closet-sized, windowless supply room, where we were left to fend for ourselves. We were lucky though. The rest of the dimly lit ward was strewn with groaning expectant mothers queued up on trolleys and begging for attention. Moments after the departure of Nurse Ratched, Nancy lay back and screamed out. I could see the top of the baby's head. The infant was trying a push for freedom, and it seemed certain that if I didn't get immediate assistance, then I'd be delivering the little creature myself. Reluctantly I dashed out to find the old bag of a midwife as it appeared that she was the only one working in the maternity ward at that time.

She was at her desk, reading, when I burst into her office, yelling: 'Put the book down! The baby is coming out! Hurry up!'

She knew I was very serious about what was happening, so in a flash, she got her act together and rushed back to the ward. In the time it took Dave Casbolt to down a pint, the newest member of our family slithered into the world in one slick movement. As opposed to the prolonged, painful birth that Nancy had endured when Sam was born, all it took was one push to eject a nine-and-a-half-pound monster. On 9 March 1988, national non-smoking day, our second son, Bobby, was born yapping and gurning. He didn't stop for the next six months, but I wouldn't have swapped being a father to my beautiful boys for anything in the world.

This was a period of time that was not without complication. In between the births of our children, the natural order of things took a severe body swerve. Willie Wilson had been more active than usual as he went about his clandestine affairs, dressing in fine suits and being whisked away in large cars by dubious-looking wise guys. Most of Willie's dodgy dealings were directly related to a consultation with someone on the inside at Lambourn Stables, where the informant would leak enough to give him a slight edge against the big bad bookmaker.

On this occasion though, he was saying nothing, and as a result, that made it all the more mysterious. One thing was certain: it would almost surely not end well. After a few weeks of the unexplained comings and goings, Willie called in for a brief visit to see Nancy and me. He was on edge and didn't say much but left us with a cryptic assertion that we would benefit financially if his upcoming project went according to plan. With that, he was on his way down the road, marching at a high pace. He was always up to no good, so we brushed it aside, expecting him to be broke soon and asking for a loan instead of paying anything out.

Then we got the news. Willie had been scooped up during a joint Special Branch–FBI sting at the Post House Hotel, trying to convert 250,000 pounds of forged 50-dollar bills to pounds sterling. His dim-witted partner had taken them both to the hotel, driving his own taxi. A surveillance unit had been following their every move, and as Willie approached the supposed contact with a suitcase stuffed full of dollars, he was nabbed. Someone had tipped the authorities off about the fraudulent operation, and they were caught red-handed. They were taken to the police station and charged with attempting to transfer the counterfeit bills.

At that time, this type of activity had been occurring in various locations throughout the UK. Certain towns were selected by the big knobs behind the scenes, and local petty criminals were approached to act as runners. With the promise of up to ten grand as a reward for acting as the middle man, these mugs were not hard to find. Each charge had a potential five-year stretch in prison for the offenders if found guilty, which was just what Willie's sidekick got. And once again, Willie's wheeling and dealing enabled him to get a lighter sentence. He dragged Ena and Nancy around with him to back him as he convinced a string of neurologists that he was in the early stages of Alzheimer's.

And it worked. He was sentenced to two years in prison as opposed to the original five. His time inside freed Ena up to have a new lease on life as she, along with her two friends, danced the night away each weekend without any fear of Willie going on in her ear. That all ended upon his release, and with the cancellation of the fun-filled nights, she slipped back into the old routine.

CHAPTER 26

THE FINAL WHISTLE

Parenthood was the final dispersing of the crowd and the curtain call for our wayward ways. Some of us still hit the bricks on a Friday night for a few jars, but it would never be the same.

I still had one more excursion with the football team to complete before I called it a day. As I was club captain, they needed me to lead our table-topping team to make a name for ourselves in Portugal. Naz, a competent centre back, was engaged to a girl of Portuguese descent. He had arranged a match against a junior side of Quarteira, a club from the second division in the National League. The team was situated on the sunny Algarve coast, so it would make a pleasant change from competing in grimy Belgian towns. It had been a good start to the season for local football in Reading. We had lost just one game and sat in a strong position at the top of the third division of the Combination League. Reading FC was on a record-breaking run in the English third division. They had won ten games on the trot and seemed unbeatable.

We flew to Faro, feeling quite upbeat. Two players had pulled out at the last minute, but we felt that the twelve-man squad was strong enough for a successful campaign. The flight was smooth, and the accommodation was first class. We relaxed on the first day by kicking back at the beach and riding the giant breakers on a surfboard purchased between each team member. The board was left against a wall in the town centre after we got fed up carting it from bar to bar.

And as in true British fashion, the evening was a complete write-off due to our overindulging in a few vats of Mateus rosé.

The next day, suffering from a severe collective hangover, the team wakened and attempted to condition itself for the afternoon game. Individually, we were wrecks, but together we would be strong—or so we hoped. We arrived at the neat compact stadium well in advance of the kick-off in order to get a feel for the playing surface and limber up. That was the plan, but in reality, all we got the feel of was the changing room floor. One by one we crashed out for a snooze after guzzling back the water-filled containers supplied by our visitors as we hoped to regain some sort of normalcy. Later as we roused ourselves from our zombie-like state, the need for more water was now greater than ever as our throats began to close over. Eric, a midfield partner with a little less speed than me grabbed an empty flagon and went to refill it from an outside tap. He opened the changing room door, paused, and then abruptly slammed it shut.

Sporting a look of concern, he spun around on his heels and commented: 'Boys, get over here and have a butcher's.'

One by one we curiously sidled to the doorway. Eric partially cracked the door to reveal that the adjacent main stand was a hive of activity. To our left, the turnstiles were spinning and clicking as a line of spectators shuffled their way towards the section behind the goal. What was occurring? Maybe the locals loved their football so much that they came out in droves even to watch the junior sides. That was not the case though. It was evident that the crowd was not Portuguese but that it was almost without a doubt English. The ensemble marched in, exposing burnt red beer bellies and sporting hankies on their heads that indicated that they were certainly not native. Consequently, the constant chanting of 'You're gonna get your fucking head kicked in!' confirmed that they were in fact lager louts from Blighty.

Once again, the door was slammed shut as we contemplated the unusual goings-on. The acoustics began to ramp up outside, as did the feeling of anxiety the longer we remained hidden in our shelter. Tension was high, and the sound of a marching band did nothing to subdue our unease. A loud bang on the door caused us to jump back a few paces before a voice exclaimed that we had ten minutes to take to the pitch. I picked up a ball and began bouncing and catching it a few times before turning to the lads and summoning them to advance forward into the fray.

Dazzling sunlight flashed across our faces, temporarily blinding us as we marched from the changing room. Upon regaining 20/20 vision, we saw at least two thousand rabid fans whistling and chanting in expectation. I kept on walking at a steady pace, followed by my stunned teammates, as we avoided the trumpeters and side drummers parading from the centre circle. Just what was happening? The lean and athletic opposition had already lined up along the touchline; they stood to attention as they awaited our imminent arrival. A rotund character with a bushy moustache thrust a microphone close to my jaw as a cameraman banked his tripod into position in an effort to catch a shot of the visiting team from Reading.

Marching band? TV cameras? What was occurring? It was chaos! I was being interviewed in Portuguese and had no idea what this semi-celebrity was trying to say to me. An official in an Adidas tracksuit instructed us to line up next to the intimidating muscular home team. Their team captain then wheeled around to offer me his hand and present me with a silk pennant displaying the club's logo. I gratefully accepted the token of friendship, but with nothing to donate in return, I had to absorb my counterpart's look of disdain as he turned away. We lined up in position, ready to go head to head with the mighty Quarteira.

The lack of support for the local lads was obvious, whereas we seemed to be overly represented with the constant chants of 'Reading! Reading!' which echoed throughout the ground. Although baffled by this unexpected backing, we were sure it would enhance our performance. The whistle blew for kick-off, and within seconds, we were 1–0 down. None of us had moved. We were rooted firmly to our starting positions, barely able to see the white flash of opposition shirts flying past. Our mental preparation was not exact, and we were not too despondent by the sluggish start, so we prepared ourselves for a more positive challenge. After fifteen minutes, it was 4–0, and by half-time, it was 9–0.

The whistle blew for the break, and the band took to the field along with a very irate opposition coach, who began ranting and raving at our bench. What had we done? They had quite a healthy lead, and unless we had a cunning second half plan, they seemed to have possibly wrapped the contest up. Apparently, our first-half tactics, which included hanging on to the opposition's backs or kicking them up in the air as they zoomed past, displeased their coaching staff. We were knackered. What else was there to do?

A ten-minute interlude in the changing rooms was a welcome reprieve, but not long enough. We replenished our drained fluids by gulping back pints of water and the odd beer. It did not seem worth playing the second half, but it had to be done. We were in the business of entertaining, and we'd certainly done that. To make matters worse, our only sub had done a runner, as he was clearly terrified of having to come on at some point. Exhausted even though we'd hardly had any possession of the ball, we began the second half against a completely different team. The first forty-five minutes had been played against a full squad of professionals from the Portuguese second division, and that was the reason why the coach had been bouncing about in anger. He was concerned that one of his superstars might have been injured, and so he decided to send out the reserve team for the second half. With twenty minutes left and down 11–0, we lost a player to injury, leaving us with ten men, so the chances of netting a few quick goals to get level were now slim.

At one point, a volunteer from the crowd jumped the fence, apparently ready to fill in on the wing. It was of little consequence that this interloper was not a club member, as we were a spent force, and we figured that another body might just help ease the pain. He ambled on to the pitch with the grace of a knock-kneed giraffe and a gait like John Cleese in the *Ministry of Silly Walks*. The sideshow did not disappoint anyone. On his very first involvement, he'd banged his noggin on the ground and was knocked out cold after falling over his own feet as he attempted to get his stick insect legs in motion. The medical staff scooped the five-minute wonder on to a stretcher and took him out of the ground for further treatment.

When the final whistle sounded, the score had peaked at 16–0. The mumbling crowd dispersed, not sure of what they had witnessed, but they were not as shell-shocked as we were. Usually, a little research went into finding an opposition with similar attributes to ourselves, but this was a non-contest. We eventually discovered that the fiasco could be traced back to a simple translation error. The local radio station had heard that record-breaking Reading FC from the English third division was to take on Quarteira from the Portuguese second division in a friendly match. This news had filtered down to the English sunseekers vacationing in the Algarve region and had attracted them to a potential first-class encounter. We'd taken a severe kicking that didn't go unnoticed by the locals. In bars, in taxis, and as we mingled with shoppers at the market, people would snigger then point and call to us, 'English, ha ha, 16–0!' The Portuguese expedition was certainly one to forget.

Back home, the wild days were now over. Change was in the air as we struggled to make ends meet whilst caring for our children. Nancy and I had one final move in Reading, to a house in Circuit Lane just off the Bath Road. We were to have some great times there, though we were now feeling a bit disillusioned about a future in Reading. After a holiday to see family in Canada, we mulled over the idea of a temporary move there if I could obtain a work permit. Then on 17 July 1989, without any warning, Ena died. The shock was severe. Just two days before, she had played with Sam and Bobby in the back garden of our house and enjoyed a meal before heading off for an evening out. She had a stroke the next morning and, after a slight recovery, passed away the following day at the Royal Berkshire Hospital.

She was the bond that tied everything together, and each of the family conditioned themselves to deal with the loss in their own unique way. Their world changed when Ena died, and we knew that things would never be the same again. Nancy and I hesitantly agreed to pack up our two boys and move into 16 Jesse Terrace in an effort to give Willie some support. It did not work out well. Willie seemed to think that he was the only one grieving, and this put a lot of stress on Nancy and on how she handled the loss. The two of them were constantly at each other's throats, and after six months, Nancy had had enough; she had to get out.

We knew that the first Christmas would be a difficult time for each of the family, so I booked a holiday cottage in Norfolk just to be away from Reading over the festive season. Willie had organised a trip to Madeira that coincided with the arrival of the *QE2* cruise liner with Tom as one of its passengers. It was a known fact that Tom rarely left the sanctuary of the Reading area, though on this occasion he thought he should get out of town. It was a big step boarding the ship and sailing off into the sunset, but this trip proved to be one too many for Tom. Less than an hour after leaving Southampton, a crazy arsonist set fire to one of the cabins; it spread out into the corridor and caused the ship to drop anchor whilst the emergency was addressed.

For two days, Tom bobbed up and down in the St George's Channel, enjoying a somewhat-stationary view of the Hampshire coast. When the liner did eventually set sail again, the itinerary was altered with the cancellation of visits to certain islands, and this caused the ship to arrive late in Madeira. This delay created a mix-up with where and when Willie and Tom were supposed to meet. Of course, Willie blamed Tom for the inconvenience. As for Tom, his travelling days were well and truly over.

In the new year, we moved back to Circuit Lane, but not having Ena around left a dark cloud above our heads as we tried to carry on raising the kids with a positive attitude. To no longer see Ena's beaming face or hear her welcoming distinctive voice again was hard to bear, so we prepared to take the giant step and leave England. In February 1990, I flew to Toronto for an interview with Kone Elevators, and within two months, the work papers arrived. The application to enter Canada on a two-year work permit was successful, and if we had second thoughts before, we were now sure since Ena's passing. We rented our house to a couple from Liverpool in preparation for an excursion into the unknown.

During my recent trip to Toronto, I had witnessed a karaoke act for the first time and thought that it would be a great way to highlight the evening of our going-away party. The problem was that no one in England had ever heard of karaoke. Numerous calls to various radio stations and entertainment organisations had people baffled. One company thought we were looking to hire someone to teach us a martial art, and another suggested that karaoke was a type of seafood served with rice. Finally, we reached someone who knew what we were talking about.

A girl at Capitol Radio in London put us in touch with Laser Karaoke, the only existing karaoke franchise in England at that time. They were part of a BBC children's programme production and had only just set up the travelling karaoke team. As no one in the UK had any idea what they were all about, it was difficult to advertise their product, and they were keen to be part of our farewell show. Nancy and I wanted the act, but it would be expensive. They required 500 pounds for the night, which was a lot more than we could really afford. We came to an agreement that they would use the night as a big promotional event to get their name out for the lowly sum of 350 pounds. It was still expensive, but we went for it.

For our swansong, we had rented the Reading Rowing Club on the banks of the Thames. Only Eugene and Muff knew of the karaoke surprise, though they were not too sure what to expect. The three of us went to the club to help set up and distribute the song sheets to each table. By 8 p.m. most of the arrivals had positioned themselves in the back bar, oblivious to the sound checks and mic tapping occurring at the far end of the main hall. A few curious couples browsed the karaoke pages that accompanied each table. By 9 p.m. the main hall was like a ghost town. I could not drum up any interest from the back bar to check out the karaoke crew that patiently awaited the arrival of the first crooner.

I turned to Eugene and Muff and said, 'Look, one of us is going to have to get up there and sing, or I've just wasted 350 quid.'

They both looked nervous as they came to terms with the drastic measures that would have to be taken to save the day. It would have been drastic if either of them was to sing as it would be a certain GBH of the earholes. Then I asked Julie to use her charm in an effort to entice the hard-seasoned drinkers out of the back bar. She confronted Tom, the ringleader, hoping that if she could get him out, the rest would follow.

'Tom, come on out and do the karaoke,' she pleaded.

He replied, 'No chance. I'm not doing the bloody hokey-cokey for anybody.'

Then there was a breakthrough. Big Chris and his girlfriend kicked off the proceedings with an awful attempt at 'You're the One that I Want'. They were an instant hit and became the catalyst to encourage another act to step forward. Next up were the exotic Caribbean sisters Pam and Carol, who livened the place up with 'Wanna Dance with Somebody'. Malcolm and Jackie soon followed to serenade the sparse main hall crowd with 'Endless Love'. One by one the back-bar brigade inquisitively eased out and slowly made their way out into the hall. Soon it was a free-for-all. The list to take a turn behind the mic steadily increased as individual, duo, and multi-person acts took to the stage. Tom McLenaghan was in excellent voice, singing 'Teddy Bear', as was Nick Milsom with 'Addicted to Love'. The Dave-and-Greg duo dreadfully performed 'Livin' Doll', and when Derry Gerry destroyed 'The Heat is On', the Laser staff plugged their ears with cotton wool. Other notable acts included 'It's Not Unusual' by Muff, sporting twenty Marlborough in his trouser pocket and twenty in his shirt pocket, and Eugene, who belted out his version of 'What Do You Want?' Pete the Cheat then excelled with 'Daydream Believer', delivering it with impeccable timing and getting the rapturous crowd to sing along. He never flinched during a constant barrage of sandwiches and sausage rolls that bounced off his mush.

The stars of the night were without doubt Nancy and Julie, who performed what was meant to be their one and only song, 'It's My Party'. We could not get these two off the stage as they warbled on and on despite the anxious punters waiting in the wings with limited time left on the clock. I finished the evening off with an enchanting melodic version of 'Ob-La-Di, Ob-La-Da'. A piece of history was made in Reading that night with what was certainly the first karaoke performance in Berkshire, if not the tropical south of England. By evening's end, people were left disappointed and unable to get their moment in the spotlight because of the archaic British licensing laws. God said that no drink could be served after midnight as it would be a sacrilege to serve alcohol in the early hours of the Lord's Day. As we were about to leave the club, Gerry presented Nancy and me with an unexpected bonus to the evening's jovialities. He had recorded the entire karaoke performance on videotape as a fond reminder of our last night in Reading in the company of great friends. With mixed emotions, we said our final goodbyes to the people who had been a constant presence in our lives for so long.

The period that we enjoy between our late teens and mid twenties does not seem to have any consequences. We are too busy enjoying the moment. There is nothing to lose, so why should we not live on the edge without having to worry about the insignificant factors of life? Those days rapidly fly past, and before we know it, the tentacles of time have taken hold. You begin to follow the manual of adulthood. You do what everyone else does.

A few short years before, I had arrived in Reading, full of hope and excitement; I hadn't known anyone or anything about the town or its people. Before long, I was part of the community, living life to the extreme and being made to feel welcome and at ease by my new friends as my troublesome Belfast days became a distant memory. But all things must pass, and the cycle of youth soon faded. Then the next stage began. It was a domino effect. From meeting a girl to finding the first flat and then buying a house and, in the end, getting married. It was never planned; it just happened.